Teaching a Man to Fish
by Raising Chickens

Teaching a Man to Fish
by Raising Chickens

To: Pat Cramer,
Please enjoy this book &
thank you for your kind attention
Marvin J. Schuttloffel
9-11-14

MARVIN J. SCHUTTLOFFEL

iUniverse, Inc.
Bloomington

Teaching a Man to Fish by Raising Chickens

iUniverse books may be ordered through booksellers or by contacting:

iUniverse
1663 Liberty Drive
Bloomington, IN 47403
www.iuniverse.com
1-800-Authors (1-800-288-4677)

ISBN: 978-1-4620-6672-8 (sc)
ISBN: 978-1-4620-6674-2 (hc)
ISBN: 978-1-4620-6673-5 (ebk)

Library of Congress Control Number: 2011960854

Printed in the United States of America

iUniverse rev. date: 11/11/2011

CONTENTS

To all the Papal Volunteers who gave a portion of themselves with little or no publicity;
To my mother, Lucille, who saved all of the letters I wrote, a treasure trove for this publication;
To my father, who inspired me for a life of service;
To Mimi, my loving wife of thirty-eight years, who encouraged me to write this book;
To my wonderful sons, lovely daughters-in-law, and all of my beautiful and brilliant grandchildren.

Give a man a fish, and you feed him for a day.
Teach a man to fish, and you feed him for a lifetime.

Chinese Proverb

CHAPTER 1

ON AN IOWA FARM

In the early spring of 1964, my second-oldest brother, Joseph, asked me to accompany him to a meeting in Remsen, Iowa. Iowa men who wanted to see slides of the Papal Volunteers to Latin America (PAVALA) filled the small parish basement. A priest who had a sibling in the program presented the slides. He did a marvelous job of explaining the work, challenges, and rewards of working along the Amazon River in Brazil. The priest informed us that Papal Volunteers was started at a Eucharistic Congress held in Rio de Janeiro in 1955. The bishops of Latin America sought outside help to get the Church to return to her original strength and vigor. They appealed to Rome for a solution. Pope Pius XII, accordingly, established the Pontifical Commission for Latin America to study and present a workable plan. Step six of the findings called for a substantial increase in the role of the lay apostolate. In the summer of 1960, Pope John XXIII signed the first document entitled "Papal Volunteers for Apostolic Collaboration in Latin America."

The first part of the program was to have more religious clergy made available to Latin American needs. Each religious order was requested to send more of its own. The second part of the appeal involved having a program directed to the laity of the world, particularly those of the United States and Canada. Thus began a massive lay movement in an all-out effort to save a substantial membership of the Mystical Body of the Catholic Church. On January 15, 1961, Cardinals Cushing and Meyer sent a joint letter to the bishops of the United States, requesting that a two-pronged program be founded on the same basic principles. It was to be a united effort at the diocesan level. The appeal was placed in the charge of a lay

1

volunteer representative, a priest who would act as a promoter, recruiter, screener, and placement director of lay volunteers. The Most Reverend Joseph M. Mueller, bishop of the Diocese of Sioux City, initiated a program under the title of the "lay apostolate."[1]

The priest explained that Papal Volunteers were fulfilling a special commitment for three years, teaching the poor of Brazil their specific trades and talents. The whole concept of the Papal Volunteers was to work themselves out of a job in three years. The commitment of the Papal Volunteers was not to be missionaries, but rather ambassadors to our Church and from our country. Monetary support came from the Catholic dioceses of particular states, and the priest recruited for the Diocese of Sioux City, Iowa. And as it turned out, he was pretty good at it too.

Somewhere during the presentation I attended, the priest paused and asked, "Is there anyone who is willing to hear more details about the Papal Volunteers?"

Four people raised their hands, and the priest asked them to come into another room. Bear in mind, I only had my hand up to accompany my brother in his interest.

The priest started with the two young ladies in the room. "How old are you?"

A young lady replied, "Eighteen."

The priest quickly replied, "See you in three years!"

The same thing happened to the next girl, who was nineteen.

The priest reminded us, "Twenty-one is the minimum to serve in Brazil." His eyes fell on my brother Joseph. He knew Joseph appeared old enough. "Are you ready to join?"

My brother said, "I want to think it over."

Without hesitation, the priest turned to me. "Are you interested?"

"Yes!"

He shook my hand. "Congratulations! We have another Papal Volunteer!"

Flabbergasted, I blurted out, "But I'm not twenty-one either, Father!"

---

[1] As the success of the program grew, Cardinal Cushing presented this new concept to President John F. Kennedy, who used the concept as a rationale to create the Peace Corps.

His face just fell. "How old are you?"

"Twenty."

The priest had renewed hope. "When is your birthday?"

"I'll turn twenty-one on July 19."

The priest let out a delighted gasp. "No problem. You'll be twenty-one before you leave American soil, so congratulations! We have another Papal Volunteer."

He pumped my hand until I thought he wanted to keep it. I was stunned and speechless as I looked at Joseph, who was grinning widely. I could tell he wasn't going to help me get out of it. The rest of the time spent with the priest was a jumbled blur of words as he provided information. My mind was racing like a racecar gone mad careening around a crowded track. I could see the caution and stop flags whipping out in front of me. I just kept going faster and faster.

On the way home, Joseph just kept up the one-liners and continued to burst into laughter. The trip was only about twenty miles, but it seemed to take hours.

What and how am I going to tell my parents?

I wasn't too sure of this myself, much less convince my parents that it was a good idea that I, their youngest son, go to the Amazon Rainforest for three years without any visits home. I was going to teach farming, for heaven's sake!

Joseph and I crept into the pitch-black house. I was thankful to hear Dad's loud snoring as I headed for the upstairs.

Suddenly Mom, who awoke, asked, "How was the meeting?"

Joseph couldn't contain himself any longer and burst out laughing. The loud snoring stopped abruptly, and Dad asked the same question.

"Go ahead and tell them, Marvin," my brother urged.

I grasped the dining room table for fortification and weakly proclaimed, "I'm going to Brazil as a Papal Volunteer."

The bedroom light popped on, and both my parents bolted into the living room, wide-awake.

Dad looked at me. "What did you say?"

By this time, I realized what I had said, and it seemed like the right thing to say. Mom's eyes welled up with tears, as they were prone to do when dealing with me. Both were trying to accept the idea that I would be going three thousand miles away from home, and they knew I had never been too far from home. After about thirty minutes of interrogation, Dad waved us off to bed, where the three of us got very little sleep. Joseph slept soundly.

—⁓⁌⁍⁖⁘⁙⁚⁛—

As a lad, I was very lucky to have my parents. My dad was always proud of his family of seven children. Jerry, the oldest, next Joseph, then my sister Marge, my one year older brother, Bob, my twin brother Darwin, and finally, my little sister, Mary Jo. I was the youngest of a set of twins and the baby of the family until my sister Mary Jo arrived nine years after my birth.

Dad struggled to make a living on a 160-acre farm in northwestern Iowa. He never owned any brand-new equipment, nor did he ever have a new car in his life. He frequented farm sales and bought equipment to replace the old junk. When he brought something home, it usually needed a complete overhaul before we could use it. His equipment needed constant repair, but he could—and did—fix anything and everything. With his guidance, his boys learned to be very innovative as well, and I believe that being poor never hurt us mentally. With most everything needing repairs, all of the boys in the family were quite good mechanics and carpenters and became especially knowledgeable about livestock.

Being born and raised on a farm was the best life anyone could hope for. Even though life was difficult at times, all of us worked hard together to survive. We used everything the land yielded from the farm to feed fifteen milk cows. Their offspring were then raised, fattened, and sold on the market. Of the two hundred chickens, half were egg-producing hens. The remainders were roosters, some of which my mother butchered and canned for later consumption. We butchered and sold the remainder of the roosters to nearby neighbors.

With Joseph's constant input and work, we also fed brood sows to produce nearly five hundred head of hogs annually that we sold for slaughter. On the land itself, we raised mostly corn, alfalfa for hay, and small grains, such as oats and sorghum.

Our house was built in the early 1900s and only had small oil stoves to heat the rooms. The kitchen, where Mom did all her cooking and baking, was kept nice and toasty with her corncob/wood burning stove. I can still smell and taste her homemade bread and yummy cinnamon rolls.

Three bedrooms were on the upper portion of the house, where no heat was ever provided, no matter how cold it got during the winter. Sometimes when it got really cold, my twin brother, Darwin, Bob and I, who all slept in the same bed, would pre-warm the pages of a Sears and Roebuck catalog and take it to bed. We'd put them down by our feet to help warm us.

When the wind blew while it snowed, Dad would call at six in the morning, "Boys, it's time to get up!"

We'd jump out from under the heavy covers, and our feet would land right into a snow bank that had drifted through the cracks of the window frames during the night. Needless to say, we quickly put on our winter clothes. We rose early every day because all of us had chores before we headed off to school.

And weekends were no exception. Because of all the things Dad needed our help with, he saved them for Saturday and Sundays, and of course, we had church on Sundays. We had to milk the cows by hand, clean the milk cow stalls, and process the milk through a cream separator right after milking. We fed some whole milk to the calves, the offspring of the milk cows. We fed the skimmed milk to the pigs. The chickens and, of course, the dog had to be fed. I was personally in charge of feeding the rabbits we raised for food. I also had to make sure we had corncobs to keep the kitchen stove going.

Off to school we went in our hand-me-downs. My mom had to patch some of the clothes to last through five boys.

When I complained about it, Mom would counter, "The clothes might be patched, but at least they're clean."

My shoes weren't hand-me-downs because I had to wear a special elevated shoe. My left foot was two sizes smaller than the right was, and the same leg was over an inch shorter than the right leg was. My parents could only afford one pair of shoes for me, so I had to try to clean the cow crud off them before I went to school or church. The hardest time to get them clean was in the spring when everything was muddy and slick. I could tell the days I didn't do a very good job, because the girls at school would wrinkle their noses and give me a wide berth.

Mom worked the hardest of all, in my estimation. During the winter, she would sew all of our clothes, including our underwear, shirts, and pants. She kept our socks mended, scrubbed the floors by hand on her knees, and drove us everywhere we had to go. As a teenager, I sure hoped no one at school would see some of the patterns of my boxer-style shorts. I pined for just one pair of tighty-whitey briefs, but it never happened.

The chickens were Mom's responsibility, but we were instructed how to feed them and gather the eggs. Mom would wash each and every egg before packing them in cardboard crates of thirty dozen. When the crate was full, Mom would haul them to town on the way to school. She would sell them at the local creamery and use that cash for groceries and school supplies. With what was left, Mom would buy sewing materials for more clothes. We also earned money from the cream we had gleaned from milking the cows, and we also sold it to the local creamery.

During the summer, Mom would have the biggest garden around, and she tilled the soil, planted the vegetables, and weeded and watered the garden. When the time came in the fall, Mom would be canning for weeks.

With all the farm work going on, Dad would keep everyone busy with a multitude of tasks, such as baling hay, hoeing weeds by hand, fixing fences, cleaning livestock barns, and so forth. When Mom needed an extra hand in the house, I was usually chosen. I know I was Mom's favorite son.

All my brothers served in some branch of the military, and I knew I could never pass the physical because of my short leg. That bothered me. I wanted to contribute, and when the opportunity came to serve in the Papal Volunteers, I knew this was the chance of a lifetime.

CHAPTER 2

SCHOOL IN SIOUX CITY

Iowa weather in April usually has its ups and downs, and that was pretty well the way I felt that whole month. Fear crawled inside my brain. Every time I tried to confront it, it would slip away like a shy dog, hiding but always lurking about. But on occasion, I'd feel just a fleeting glimpse of it. The best time I had with my decision was when I got to talk about it and explain what I wanted to do. In early May, the Chancery Office of the Diocese of Sioux City, Iowa, sent me a letter with my marching orders, so to speak. I was to report to Sioux City on July 1 and meet the two other Papal Volunteers that same Sunday afternoon at four o'clock at our new residence, formerly a caretaker's house in Calvary Cemetery.

Because I had never been to Sioux City, I took off early with a four-time hand-me-down 1947 Chevy that we fondly called the "Tank." Glued on the sun visor were the insignia patches of the tank division that my oldest brother, Jerry, had sent us from Germany, where he served in the army. The "Tank" consumed a quart of oil every hundred miles, and the gas mileage wasn't that great either. I packed everything in the car that I felt I would need, including bed sheets, towels, and clothes, but I didn't have any food.

When I arrived early at the cemetery, I parked under a mulberry tree heavily laden with berries. Next to it stood a rundown structure that was going to be home for the next three and a half months. Four o'clock came and went. By six, I was starving. I found the house to be locked and empty. No one was around to ask for advice or directions to the nearest fast-food stop. By seven, I had pretty well stripped all the lower branches of the black, ripened mulberries. By eight, I made another round on the tree and devoured all the nearly and not-so-ripe berries. By nine, I was up in the tree with a flashlight searching ever so carefully for any more berries. Around ten, a taxi pulled up. From it emerged my new companions with their supplies, a key to the house, and, most importantly, a few groceries. After three peanut butter sandwiches, I made my bed and retired, not too happy, but I felt the crisis was over. Boy was I was wrong! About two in the morning, I had a gastronomical event and again at three and four, and by five, I was literally cleaned out.

John, the new volunteer was from Milwaukee and the oldest in the group at the age of thirty-eight. He had army experience, so he set the agendas and doled out the rules for every function in order to run an efficient household. John, a no-nonsense kind of person, took his role quite seriously. He had been a radio operator in the army, and he was to establish communication up and down the Amazon by equipping the Redemptorist Fathers' boats with shortwave radios.

The other volunteer, Bob, was much younger at just barely twenty-one years old. He was from Carroll, Iowa, and he didn't have any definite plans on what he was going to do in Brazil. He just knew he wanted to go there and contribute. He had a great sense of humor, took life really lightly, and loved a good time.

On Monday, John got us organized and immediately laid down the ground rules. We had rules for everything from how the cooking would be done, who would then do the dishes, and how and when things were to happen. He forgot nothing. All three of us were due at the Chancery Office at eleven in the morning that day, so with me at the wheel of the Tank, John in the front seat scanning the city map, and Bob in the backseat hanging on for dear life, we started off.

When we arrived at the office, it was well after the time we were expected. We had gotten lost and saw a fair amount of the city. At the meeting, Father Raymond Kevene, director of the Papal Volunteers for the Diocese of Sioux City, laid out the next three months of activities. He explained we would be attending Briar Cliff College in the evening to study Portuguese under the direction of Dr. De La Compa. Bob and I would have a job at St. Vincent's Hospital doing whatever needed to be done under the direction of the engineering department. John landed a job at the Emerson Radio assembly plant right outside of the city. He would have the Tank throughout the day. This was my first job ever, and luckily, I had just received my Social Security card the week before.

At St. Vincent's, the staff in the engineering department was great to us and showed a lot of patience and latitude. As it happened, the department really did need us. The hospital was being remodeled, and we were to fill in the top windows above all the doors with Sheetrock so the ceilings in the hallways could be lowered. Two hundred and forty rooms were on the four levels. Bob, a real cutup with a personality that everyone liked, learned the ins and outs of each patient as we were in each room on each floor. In the meantime, I climbed the stepladder, measured the windows, cut the Sheetrock, and put each new addition back in.

Bob kept me and the boys in the engineering department entertained with his stories. For a naïve farm boy with the corn sticking out my ears, some of the stories Bob gleaned from the patients were unreal.

Ambrose (Am), one of the engineers, decided to clean out the boiler room coffeepot, which hadn't been cleaned for a year. The pot had a lot of sludge, as Am put it. So one day, he filled the coffeepot with muriatic acid, a solution designed to be mixed with water and used to clean the huge air-conditioner coils of their lime buildup. Am used the solution full strength in the aluminum percolator, plugged it in, and proceeded to work in another room. When Am and the rest of us stopped working and returned to the boiler room for a break and a cup of coffee, only the cord and part of the spout was left. The remaining parts had melted to nothing, all eaten by the acid. We just howled as the red-faced Am scanned the caution label of the muriatic acid, which spelled out in bold letters, "Do Not Use on Aluminum."

Our Spanish professor, a refugee from the Cuban crisis, was a scholarly man in medicine and held the title of doctor, but he couldn't practice medicine because he couldn't be certified in the United States. The diocese hired this gentleman who could hardly speak English and had one of the thickest Spanish accents ever to teach the three of us Portuguese. When we landed in Brazil, we couldn't even say good morning or good evening correctly, much less ask, "Where is the bathroom?" God bless the good doctor, he really tried, and we studied hard under the stern, watchful eye of John.

Then a famous soccer athlete, Raul Vilhena, from Manaus, Brazil, rescued us. He had been in an automobile accident and injured both tendons of his legs. He had to wear heavy spring-loaded braces that would help in raising his feet as he walked. He seemed to be doomed to never play again. This poor Brazilian was brought to the States for a miracle

9

operation, and he stayed with us at the cemetery while he waited for the series of operations to transpire. Raul was a lot of fun and really hit it off with Bob and me. He taught us a lot of Portuguese, much of which couldn't be used in polite settings.

Raul and Bob would spend a lot of time walking around among the tombstones at night in search of the beer parties that often transpired there. One particular Saturday, while walking around with the two of them, we watched a crew moving a coffin right after a graveside service. Apparently, this happened fairly often. A graveside service was held at one location, and the casket was then moved to its final resting place. This crew loaded the casket in the utility jeep and proceeded up a very steep grade. Suddenly, we heard one of the crew members yell for the driver to stop. We watched in disbelief as the casket tumbled out of the jeep and rapidly rolled all the way down the hill with the burial crew in hot pursuit. Finally, the casket stopped rolling, and the crew calmly reloaded the casket on to the jeep and headed off again.

The calmness in which the crew handled the situation made me wonder to myself, Just *how many times does this happen?*

As school progressed and time passed in Sioux City, our departure approached. I worried about my expertise in farming, which was strictly on-the-job training that my father's orders had guided during my teen years. Looking back, that was the best training I could have had. Due to everyone's lack of knowledge of what was happening fifteen hundred miles up the Amazon, including the School of Agriculture at Iowa University, no one had an idea of what type of farming techniques I would need. No one realized I had the perfect preparation.

John, the organizer and planner for the three of us, designed a plan to build wooden trunks to ship our goods to Brazil. So in our spare time, we worked on this project as well as studied Portuguese and kept house. One useless item that took up a lot of trunk space was expensive rain gear. We purchased very heavy coal black raincoats, boots, and rain hats, a huge mistake because of the humidity and temperature. When we wore this outfit, we were drenched with sweat on the coat's underside. We scared the hell out of the native children. Among other things packed in the trunk were seven volumes of my dad's correspondence texts of engineering from DeVry Institute. And to my dad's disappointment, they remained in Brazil upon my return.

On August 4, 1964, we began receiving vaccinations for our stay in Brazil, intending to immunize us from typhoid, paratyphoid, polio, yellow fever, smallpox, and typhus. For me, the most painful was the typhoid-paratyphoid series that we received as a shot in the muscle of each arm. My muscles became so inflamed that it was painful to raise my arm or roll over on my side during the night. We were told this was a "good" reaction.

Raul and Bob spent a lot of time bashing John's regimented ways and schedules, and they did everything they could to rattle him. Needless to say, John became irritated very easily. This relationship cost Bob in the long run because, when it came to deciding the capability of the volunteers, John's opinion weighed heavily.

At the end of the term in Sioux City, the director of our volunteer program Fr. Kevene asked Bob to leave the program. Looking back, I think Bob would have been an asset to the program because he would have been a great influence on the Brazilian kids. Raul was to stay in the States for several needed operations. Several months later, I heard his operations had failed to relieve him of his clumsy braces. The hopes for a full recovery were dashed, and Raul entered a school of accounting in the United States. The Brazilian people are a very proud people, and this Brazilian is no exception. I can only imagine how this must have hurt Raul.

Chapter 3

My Journey to Brazil

Upon completion of our months of study in Sioux City, John and I went home on October 7. We stayed for two weeks to say good-bye to our families and prepare for our time in Brazil. Our send-off was a Mass as a celebration, and the special blessing for missionaries was bestowed on us. Each of us was given a very special crucifix with some relics of missionary saints encased inside. Even though John was from Milwaukee, which had its own Papal Volunteers, he was given the same send-off from my St. Mary's parish in Larchwood because now he represented the Diocese of Sioux City.

For years before our send-off, I had been seeing a chiropractor in Sioux Falls due to my left leg condition. Dr. Johnson was very excited about my going to Brazil, and he offered a prediction.

"You will not cry when you leave your folks and the United States, but I bet you'll cry when you leave Brazil."

On October 20, I left on a flight to Kansas City, my first leg of a long journey to Brazil. My chiropractor was right. So far, I didn't weep, but I sure wanted to as I looked down on my parents waving to me when the plane flew over them. Once in Kansas City, John joined me. I also met a new volunteer named Ann, a nurse from the Diocese of Kansas City, and our guide to Mexico, Father Lies,[2] who had a sister in the Papal Volunteers program in Brazil.

---

[2] Lease

As part of the transition process, the four of us boarded a train bound for Mexico City, where we would dedicate our next three years to God at the Shrine of Our Lady of Guadalupe. The brief experience in Mexico was to prepare us for the next three years living in a Latin American setting, using our language skills to survive, and being on our own.

The train ride through the Ozarks Mountains was breathtaking for the fall colors were at their peak. A local passenger on the train told me that the foliage was the brightest he had ever seen. I took that sign to heart for I had a warm feeling that God had a very special reason for me to see such beauty. I felt a little bit better about going to Brazil.

When the train crossed the border, we had to enter Mexico through customs. Father Lies advised us on how to act under the watchful eye of the customs agents. This was the first encounter where John and Father Lies butted heads, all because John thought he knew better. Father Lies placed his Roman collar at the very top of his open luggage, and he was waved right through even though Roman Catholic priests weren't allowed into Mexico. I was next and answered the questions as Father Lies had advised.

The Mexican border patrol agent asked John, "Do you have anything to declare?"

John laughed. "A pack of cigarettes."

The agent glared at him, picked up his open luggage, and dumped everything out, spilling the contents off the table and onto the floor. John had to pick up everything after the agent was done rummaging through them. John was furious, but Father Lies intervened before John could worsen the moment.

"Do not show any emotions of anger or say anything that would bar your entry into Mexico."

The Mexican excuse of a train was "vintage" and showed its years of wear from climbing the Guadalupe Mountains to Mexico City. The train traveled into the night, and I slept fitfully because I could feel every bump and jolt in what was termed a first-class coach. About three in the morning, I awoke but didn't see Father Lies anywhere. I left the first-class coach and walked to the second-class cars, only to find that these cars had the locals riding in them with their produce and farm animals on their way to or from the local markets. The windows in second and third class coaches were down or nonexistent, and I could understand why due to the crowded conditions and the livestock that was in the rail car with us.

13

About the third car back, I found Father Lies sitting on the hard bench, in the middle of the train, with a tub of beer steeped in ice.

Father Lies explained this was his favorite part of the trip, where he got to commune with the locals. I could tell his Spanish was pretty good as I headed back to first class where Ann and John were still asleep.

I was too excited to sleep as the train rattled its way up the mountains, and with the full moon, I only got glimpses of the beautiful landscape. Close to dawn, we seemed to level off on a valley floor. I made my way back toward Father Lies. I hung my head out of the open windows as I went by and tried to see ahead despite the coal-fired smoke bellowing back toward me. When I found him, I could tell he was smashed and still seemed to be enjoying the trip although his Spanish was quite slurry.

John, Ann, and I ate breakfast in the dining car. Right afterward, we all set out to explore our surroundings on the train. In the second-class cars, we leaned out of the open windows each time the train went through a village and stared at the women who stood by the tracks trying to sell food or trinkets. I was amazed to see the little children with their arms outstretched begging for money. Every child was cuter than the next. The sooty coal smoke filtered through the open windows into the cars and created this blue fog like haze. We didn't realize that our faces and our clothes were turning black. Talk about ring around the collar! Father Lies finally showed up as we approached Mexico City and prepared us to disembark the train and encounter the city. He explained our itinerary and how to guard our belongings and take care in choosing what to photograph.

When I first arrived at the hotel, I took a long bath and cleaned myself up because we were soon to leave for the shrine. I couldn't wait to see the famed cloak with the Virgin Mary's image that dates back to December 1531. According to traditional Catholic accounts, Juan Diego saw a vision of the Blessed Virgin. During the vision, the Virgin asked Juan to have a church built at that very site and to name the church in her honor. When Juan spoke to the Spanish bishop, Fray Juan de Zumarraga, about the request, Bishop Fray asked for proof. Juan returned to the apparition location, and the Virgin again appeared to him. She asked Juan to gather roses from the hilltop, even though it was the dead of winter. Despite the season, Juan found Castilian roses scattered about. He brought them back to the Virgin Mary, who herself arranged them in his cloak. When Juan presented the cloak to the bishop, Juan knew only of the roses, but as the cloak unfolded, the image of the Virgin of Guadalupe miraculously appeared imprinted on the cloth of Juan Diego's cloak. This very famous cloak hangs behind the main altar and is the subject of profound faith of many of the Mexican people.

For me, the pilgrimage to the shrine seemed like the natural thing to do, and before leaving, Father Lies advised all of us how to use safety pins to secure our money, passport, and wallets in some safe place. John completely ignored Father Lies, which just annoyed the priest even more, and they came to words. John stated he had been in many situations and he never had his wallet lifted. Father Lies countered we would be in very close crowds and the thieves have been well trained over the years. Ann and I complied with Father Lies's warning and pinned our belongings where no thief dare go.

While standing outside the shrine, I couldn't believe the demonstration of faith—men and women—inching toward the shrine. Some were on their knees praying the rosary and starting as far as a block away. Some wept as they moved. Inside the shrine, Father Lies was right. The crowd was oppressive and pushed into us so hard that we lost contact with each other. I could see John and Ann over the crowd for they both were tall, but I couldn't have caught up with them if I had to. I lost sight of Father Lies, who was rather short.

The Mass was beautiful, and I was thrilled to be a part of the demonstration of faith. I was especially captivated with a glass case that contained a very badly bent crucifix. A sign was attached to the case that explained that someone in the 1930s had placed a bomb behind the crucifix on the altar, right under Juan Diego's cloak. The bomb blast hurled the heavy crucifix all the way out of the shrine and onto the plaza out front, a good full city block from the main altar. The blast caused hundreds of people to rush to the shrine, fully expecting to find the cloak of Juan Diego to be shredded, but found it unharmed instead. Shortly after the blast, a heavy plate glass shield was installed over the cloak. I couldn't help but notice that a small corner of the glass case, where the crucifix was on display, was broken out and several Mexican coins were dropped into the case.

When the four of us squeezed through the crowd and out into the plaza, Father Lies admitted that his wallet had been pick pocketed. Apparently, he had ignored his own advice on safety pins, and John took great pleasure in pulling out his own wallet, which was unguarded in his back pocket all the time. This incident, among others, did little to endear them to each other.

Part of our training from Father Lies included instructions on tipping, and he advised us to tip every time we were served. The next morning at breakfast in the hotel restaurant, after consuming about fifty cents worth of food in American dollars, I counted out the correct tip and left it on the counter for the waiter. Shortly thereafter, I heard howls of laughter between two waiters working the counter. The commotion they raised caused the restaurant manager to rush over to hush them.

What's so funny?

When I met with Father Lies later, I told him what had happened, and he laughed and explained the tip I had left amounted to about one-half cent and the coin I used to transfer the wealth was reserved strictly for beggars. From that incident forward, I learned to become a more generous tipper. We didn't get to see much more of Mexico City because we were due at the airport to fly to Miami that afternoon. Father Lies was scheduled to return to Kansas City.

Upon reentering the United States, John had another incident with the United States customs from some wisecrack and again had to repack all his belongings. We were scheduled to fly out that same evening, but, because our flight was delayed, vouchers were issued for our own rooms and meals. Even though this was the nicest hotel I had ever stayed in, I didn't sleep well. It rained heavily all night, and I really missed my family back in Iowa.

Am I doing the right thing?

The next morning, John, Ann, and I boarded the largest airliner and left the United States without incident. During the flight, the captain said we were cruising at thirty-three thousand feet. The ocean below had thousands of little white tips of water and looked very inviting for a swim. I mentioned this to the passenger next to me, and he advised me that those little white tips indicated the waves were about twenty-foot swells. My plans for a swim were suddenly dashed. About halfway through the flight, the plane landed at Santa Domingo for a short stop to refuel and exchange passengers. When the door of the plane opened, a hot blast of very hot and humid tropical air struck me.

How could I possibly stand this tropic heat for three years?

Our next stop was Caracas, Venezuela, where all the passengers disembarked the plane. We were on the ground for over an hour. We were herded into transit busses with armed guards. Some of the Americans made crude remarks about the process, and needless to say, I wasn't proud of my fellow countrymen. At this very airport, some communist guerillas had kidnapped an American pilot and were holding him for ransom. The way we were guarded was very scary, but in today's climate, it would be a piece of cake. Again, the climate seemed just as hot and humid. Safely on our way again, the stewardesses kept us well fed. For a farm lad from Iowa, I was enjoying quite the life despite the feeling of homesickness that was invading my mind and heart.

CHAPTER 4

Casa Central

Belem, Brazil

It was nearing eight at night in Brazilian time on October 29, 1964, when we landed in Belem, Brazil. We were held up until close to midnight while Father Clemente, whose official title was volunteer coordinator for the Amazon Valley, our Redemptorist connection, worked to clear up the fact that John and I had no documentation stating we had no past criminal records. While waiting, I made a long-distance call home to let everyone know I was fine. It was a strange feeling so lonely with all the activity, but I soon learned that feeling wouldn't be unusual to me, at least for a while.

Father Clemente had to stay at the airport for more arrivals as we were released from customs, which only came after the priest promised to produce the proper documents stating these foreigners were Papal Volunteers and had no criminal records. We exited the building only to find ourselves overrun with taxicab offers. With Father Clemente's aid, we picked what appeared to be the most reliable cab, and we were whisked away to Casa Central in Belem. The driver drove at a breakneck speed without the aid of headlights, and at the crest of each hill, he would turn off the ignition and coast downhill to save gas. When we approached the very narrow bridges, he would flash his headlights to gain right of way, indicating he was coming through no matter what. I said several silent prayers that the oncoming traffic would honor our taxi's challenge.

In Belem, I couldn't believe how narrow the cobblestone streets were as we sped to our new home for the next four months. When we arrived, Mother (Madre) Ventura, a very tall nun of the Order of the Precious Blood, greeted us. She was from Kansas and in charge of Casa Central, a home that owned by the Precious Blood Fathers of Germany, who conducted missionary work on the Xingu River. The good fathers used Casa Central as a retreat home and place of respite from their hard labors. The fathers permitted the schooling of foreign missionaries to learn Portuguese and adapt to the new culture of Brazil. Madre Ventura later told me that, when she had heard of this farmer coming from Iowa, she fully expected to see a much larger person than this five-foot-eight, 129-pound lightweight who stood in front of her.

My assigned room on the second level had several twin-sized beds. Mosquito netting, draped from the ceiling to the floor, covered all of the beds. A tall wardrobe stood in the corner for all the men to share for hanging things. Next to my bed stood a small dresser for my personal use. The windows to the rooms were slatted shutters, allowing for ventilation, and the floors were an unfamiliar dark hardwood. A hallway ran the length of the rooms, and looking out from the hallway, a center courtyard below was well kept with ferns and a lawn of a wide-bladed tropical grass. Directly below the men's side was the eating area and commons room. Across the courtyard was the women's side, a chapel, and the backside of Casa Central with the laundry and kitchen area. Red clay tile, which must have been original to the building, covered the roof, and the building was said to be over two hundred years old. Directly above the laundry room stood a huge cement tank for water, which a cistern filled with city water pumped full during the day. The Brazilian sun warmed the water. It didn't take long to learn the unspoken rule that, if one wanted to bathe in warm water, one would need to be first in the shower around five in the evening.

The water wasn't safe to drink until it was boiled and then filtered. I thought it strange that the water wasn't filtered first and then boiled, but I was told that boiling killed most amoebas and only by filtering the water after boiling could the liver flukes be removed. This filtering process was completed in-house with two large clay pots, stacked on top of each other, with the filter connecting them together.

Three classrooms were on the second floor in the front of the building, closest to the street. No room could be sealed from the surrounding noise of the city. The double front doors to Casa Central were quite tall, wide, very thick, and heavy with a huge door knocker to announce one's arrival for the huge doors were locked at all times. Casa Central was built over a time span of several hundred years. It was made mostly of stone, but the wood components were where time, termites, and humidity took its toll.

Neighbors were very close in that part of the city, and to one side of Casa Central, our neighbors had a flock of chickens. One barrel-chested rooster thought it was his duty to belt out the happening of the daybreak every day. The neighbor on the other side of Casa Central had guinea hens that would let out a string of earsplitting chatter regularly. Because the louvered shutters had no glass, we constantly heard the sounds of animals and traffic.

The food at Casa Central was comprised of a lot of rice and beans, but one thing particularly delightful was the fruit for a salad picked that day. It was prepared and served in large bowls that showed us a medley of fresh fruits. The pineapple was especially delicious. It could be served as a supplement to the meal or dessert. I would choose both, and I miss it yet today. And it's difficult for me to eat pineapple in the States because of its lack of natural ripening.

One day during the first week of class, I tried to undo my Portuguese training from Sioux City. I ventured out of Casa Central on my own and crossed a plaza on my way to the fort.

A man came up to me out of nowhere and asked in Portuguese, "*Que horas?*"

I stared at him as he repeated the question several times. Finally, in desperation, the man grabbed my watch-bearing arm and looked for himself.

He's trying to steal my Timex!

I recoiled with all of my strength but then realized he was asking me, "What time is it?"

The next day in class, I was the star pupil by being able to respond to our teacher's question, "How do you say, 'What time is it?'" And that pretty well relates how I learned Portuguese. Without doing well in English grammar as a student in the United States, I seemed to learn more from the street than from the books. This was fine with me for I enjoyed being with the Brazilians.

The students at Casa Central were comprised of a motley group of three different orders of nuns, two different orders of priests, and the Papal Volunteers. In addition, we had four lay teachers and a Brazilian nun, who tried their best to teach us Portuguese. Twenty-three of us were living in the house, including the staff.

> # First Letter Home
> ## November 1, 1964
>
> *Dear loved ones, my first impression of the city of Belem was "What a hole!" especially at the site of the Amazon River. The water is clay brown, and the water has a pungent odor. There are many buzzards with beet red wrinkled skins on their long necks, and they are always busy cleaning up the shoreline. But the more often I go into the streets of Belem and see the huge mouth of the Amazon, the more I like it, for it isn't so bad after all. The huge quantity of the buzzards constantly circle and land with a plop when they spot a morsel of garbage, and it's a major penalty to harm even one of these birds. The locals would turn you into the police if you did. The local people know how the stench of the city would be unbearable if it weren't for these birds. It is amazing to me to see how people bring huge woven baskets filled with garbage, balanced on their heads, and just dump it alongside the river. The buzzards, which didn't fear any man, would fly as close as seagulls in their quest for food. Foresight of the lawmakers knew that these birds performed a very important task. Despite their ugly appearance, noise, and infighting, the sanitary service they provide is invaluable. I'm surprised I don't see the common housefly like in Iowa, but plenty other insects fill in for them. I must run and get ready for class. I love you all and please, please write.*
> *Love, Marvin*

I often witnessed the buzzards and garbage process at Fort Castillo located at the Amazon's mouth, only a few city blocks from Casa Central. This location, a favorite place to find relief in the cool breezes off the Amazon, was also known for its fine cuisine. The fort was originally built to protect the mouth of the Amazon from invasion, and after centuries of its huge cannons never firing a single shot, the place was converted into a very fine dining location. All of us from Casa Central frequented the place quite often. We simply called it the "Fort."

My first dining experience occurred with Jim, one of the more versed of the Papal Volunteers on Brazilian affairs and local happenings. He invited me to join him in an evening meal at the Fort. Chiago[3] was from

---

[3] Chee-ag-o

21

the Kansas group. Chiago insisted I order the *feijoada*,[4] a rather famous dish that originated in the southeastern state of Minas Gerias in Brazil. Several kinds of sausages, inexpensive cuts of pork, black beans, and special seasoning filled the dish. The combination was very slowly cooked for days. The restaurant in the Fort was known for having the best in the city. Allegedly, all leftover table scraps from the customer's plates, no matter what type of food, was scraped into this huge bean pot and left to simmer the whole week. I was glad I took Chiago's advice because it was absolutely delicious. Still trusting his judgment, I ordered an after-dinner drink called *cacasa*, a drink derived of pure sugarcane alcohol. The drink came in a very small vile.

Is that all they serve? There's hardly a swallow in the glass.

I threw the clear liquid down my throat and immediately felt this incredible burning sensation. It was like an unbridled fire burning its way down my throat, esophagus, and into my stomach and my air passages. My whole mouth was on fire, and when I tried to breathe, I gasped for air, only to have the fire invade my lungs. I tried to look at Chiago, seeking help, but I could only see weird shapes through my tears. It took several minutes for all the pains to subside.

Finally, I croaked, "What was that?"

Chiago informed me, "You are to take very small sips over the course of time."

I never ever went near that drink again.

———

Everyone slept under mosquito nets, and at the time of my arrival, the mosquito population was at a seasonal low but with the foreboding promise that it would explode with the rainy season, which was due in about three weeks. The nets worked pretty well, but it was common to awake and see the blood-bloated bodies of several mosquitoes clinging to the inside of the net. I recognized right away that they had my own blood in them, and I couldn't help wondering if that particular insect was bearing some dread disease from the nights before. We didn't want to

---

[4]   Fay-ja-wad-a

let our minds dwell on the question of where these mosquitoes had been before invading our room.

The temperature seemed to hover around eighty-five to ninety degrees in the day, and hardly any breeze aided in the cooling. Humidity hovered around 70 to 80 percent. To find a breeze, we could take a short walk to the river's edge and usually find relief. Standing or walking in the sun seemed twenty degrees warmer. If we could walk or find work in the shade, it wasn't too bad. There didn't seem to be any dust around like back in the United States. I asked Madre Ventura about it, and she said it was too humid for dust. Any particle would draw moisture and eventually turn to mold. Every large public building—such as churches, government, and palaces—reeked of mold and was repugnant to the nose when one entered. The outside of these buildings were often a stucco of some kind and usually covered with a black fungus/mold unless the outside was cleaned and whitewashed regularly.

My first party at Casa Central was a Halloween party, and we all had a blast. A very shy Franciscan nun threw a water balloon at who she thought was a Franciscan friar. Instead, the burst balloon soaked Bishop Jude, an American bishop, also of the Franciscan order, who was working in Belem. The poor nun was so embarrassed that she hid herself in the chapel. Despite being soaked, Bishop Jude thought it was hilarious, and we laughed ourselves nearly sick, especially when the little nun was too afraid to come out of the chapel. Those fun times spent together helped stave back the feeling of loneliness that was always lurking out there somewhere, quite willing to pounce on me at any time.

It was no wonder Father Clemente warned the other volunteers, prior to my arrival, by saying, "We are getting a lad fresh off the farm in Iowa who hasn't been away from the smoke of his own chimney."

Any occasion would be a cause for a party at Casa Central. Once, Marion, a nurse and Papal Volunteer from South Dakota, secretly made a huge birthday cake for a Papal Volunteer's birthday. This wasn't an easy feat because all the ingredients had to be hand-selected from the market near Casa Central. The flour had to be sifted to get the weevils out, and the sugar had to be fresh due to the high humidity. Marion worked the night before, secretly assembling the mix and baking when no one was around. She frosted her masterpiece carefully and stored it in the pantry, hidden away for the party the next night. At the perfect moment, when all at Casa Central had sung "Happy Birthday," Marion proudly presented her product of love. It was beautiful, and all of our mouths watered for we hadn't seen, much less imagined, a cake like that, in Belem. Marion picked up the knife and began cutting. As she did, millions of tiny, clear ants poured out of the cake and spread everywhere. Huge tears spilled down her cheeks. She was inconsolable, for, in her mind, the party was ruined. But in reality, it only added to the merriment. To quote Father Clemente, "This is Brazil," as if to say, "Don't let it bother you for anything can happen."

Other occasions for parties consisted of holidays like Halloween and Christmas; someone returning to the States, coming to Brazil for the first time, or coming in from the interior; or the very reason we hadn't had a party in a while. We quickly became family to each other for we were all in the same situation, a long way from home and well out of our comfort zone.

Other undesirable guests that would appear in our bedrooms, besides the mosquitoes, were huge cockroaches the size of Matchbox cars. They'd invade every nook and cranny, and especially irritating, they loved postage stamps. They'd go after the glue on the back of the stamp but would eat the whole stamp in the process. The only solution was to store the stamps in an airtight container. The ecosystem was alive and well in Brazil, and it was nothing to see thousands of ants trying to carry off dead roaches or bugs. If bread was made without sifting the flour, we had to decide that baked bugs were protein as well or else starve.

Right beside the chapel, nestled under a fern, lived the largest frog I'd ever seen, the size of a ten-inch dinner plate. The huge frog only came out at night, and when he leapt forward, his flat, flabby stomach would make such a plop on the ceramic tile that was it was heard throughout Casa Central.

Letter to Home
November 13, 1964

Hello to everyone at home. I hope everyone is fine at home, and I'm getting pretty well settled in here at Casa Central. My teeth have been bothering me so Fr. Clemente took me to the dentist to get several teeth filled. The practice of using Novocain is nonexistent here. The dentist damned killed me. When he was drilling, I was gradually climbing out of the chair in pain. The dentist kept saying "Um memento" (wait a moment), and then he would bear down before I got away. The dentist couldn't understand English, so taking advantage of that, I cursed the dentist with a few choice American swear words. In one sitting, the dentist drilled and filled four teeth and informed me that I have two more scheduled for next Monday. While walking back to Casa Central, I purchased a key-wound, old-fashioned double-bell alarm clock for eight thousand cruzerios (or the equal of five dollars). I attended an American movie, and throughout it, I kept noticing the things of the US and saying to myself, "Oh, yes, they have that too!" as if I never lived in America. My heart skips a beat every time there is mail call for I'm so lonely to hear from somebody in the US. I was informed that mail takes at least twelve days or more to arrive from the States to Belem and much longer if the letter is going upriver. We try to send mail back to the US if someone is flying to the States and have him mail it there. Despite the fact I have been kept very busy, I miss all of you so much. Love, Marvin

---

One lay teacher, Maria, stood barely five feet tall. She had beautiful Latin eyes and a good figure. She constantly worked at getting us out on the streets to enhance our language skills. Maria once snagged an invitation to a birthday party for a friend of hers, who also turned out to be our host. This Brazilian was a very friendly and patient man who put up with our terrible Portuguese. He could play the piano with the best of them. While he proceeded to play for us, he asked for requests.

At that very moment, I had to go to the bathroom so I asked the host in my best Portuguese, "Where is the bathroom?"

Our host's face lit up, and he raised his hands as if ready to play. Then a quizzical expression clouded his brilliant smile. "Hum a few bars to get me started."

Our teacher sprang into action and, in fluent Portuguese, rescued me while all shared embarrassing laughter. From that incident, I perfected another Portuguese phrase, which I never forgot. "Sempre Que e o bathroom?

—⁓•⊙⋆⊙⊙⋆⋆⊙•⁓—

Belem was a large city, and I often set about exploring with whoever would go with me. On one particular occasion, I was with a student priest from Casa Central as we set off to the far reaches of the city. Our goal was to get to see the very large ocean port where all the big ocean liners docked to unload their wares. After spending the whole day walking, he and I tried to return to Casa Central and took what we thought to be a shortcut. We became disoriented and lost as we went deeper into the city. Then we stumbled into a part of town forbidden to us, the red-light district. Several catcalls came from scantily dressed women hanging out of their French doors. One overly endowed lady approached us with bull's-eyes painted on her huge, bare breasts. My companion muttered a prayer as I turned red-faced. We panicked and sprinted back to where we had entered the neighborhood. We finally found our way out of there.

—⁓•⊙⋆⊙⊙⋆⋆⊙•⁓—

I immediately recognized that paper was of very poor quality. Paper bags tore without much stress. Local drivers had no problem with running over someone. They had the attitude, "I have a car. Get out of the way!" One of the teachers told us that, if a person ran over someone or had an accident, he was free of all responsibilities if he eluded the police for twenty-four hours. Even if the car were abandoned at the scene, the driver could reclaim the vehicle after twenty-four hours without worry. Before going through an intersection, the driver honked his horn and proceeded without looking either way, for there were few stoplights and no stop signs. One car to one hundred people walking was the common ratio. If a car were approaching another, one vehicle simply jumped the curb onto the sidewalk. At night, cars were parked as much on the sidewalk as possible, posing a hazard. While walking, one had to step into the street in order to get around the parked cars.

Bus drivers would sometimes wait to fill their buses with passengers, and when they'd depart, they'd push the accelerator to the floor and speed to the next stop. If only one passenger were at the next stop, the bus driver would slow to about five to ten miles per hour, and that person would have to run and jump on. If one were weak of heart, those would-be riders would wait until the next bus. The exception to this method was if the passenger were a woman or more than one was waiting to board. The driver would stop then. I thought drivers might be paid by the head count.

One particular day, I was walking in downtown Belem and noticed this hunched-over, little old man crossing the two-lane street very slowly. Suddenly out of nowhere came a Volkswagen Beetle at a high rate of speed that struck the old man. The man went up on the windshield and over top of the car and was tossed high into the air. He did a full somersault and landed on his feet when he hit the ground. The impact of his landing caused the bottom of the shopping bag to explode outward, and the groceries scattered everywhere. The man stood perfectly still for a second and then slowly crumbled to the ground. When the Beetle first hit the man, there must have been dozens of witnesses, but in seconds, not a soul was around. The driver stopped for a second but then sped off. At the same time, in the distance, I could see a traffic policeman running to the scene with his whistle blowing. I dashed over to help the old man who lay groaning from his injuries. The policeman waved me away and told me in no uncertain terms to go. When I got back to Casa Central, it was explained to me that, in Brazil, the laws were such that one could be arrested for just being at the scene of an accident, and that was why everyone fled.

One of our students, a nun from Casa Central, was on a bus one night when the driver took a corner too quickly and the bus started to roll. Fortunately, a utility pole blocked the bus from going totally over. The nun's shoulder was dislocated, but at least the bus didn't roll over, and the bus company shared no liability in the matter.

Streets were mostly granite cobblestones, and the intersections, where traffic was to slow down, had speed bumps. I had never seen speed bumps before, and I made a mental note, *They should try that in the United States.*

Sidewalks were comprised of three-foot square slabs of granite usually placed two or three wide. Many of the slabs had lost their foundation from underneath so they often weren't level and protruded up, leaving a serious tripping hazard. Rain gutter openings in the streets were huge and posed a serious threat, especially because the drain opening was nine square feet. No grates were over the openings, and the gaping holes were invariably placed right at the crossings.

———·····———

In every letter to my home in Iowa, I would beg for American stamps because people traveling back to the United States could mail our letters when they landed, avoiding the Brazilian postal system and speeding up delivery by days and even weeks. I would caution my family to wipe off the glue the back for several reasons. First, because of the humidity, the stamps often arrived all pasted together. Second, the foremost reason, the cockroaches just loved the glue and would devour the whole stamp in the process. Also, I asked everyone to include a written summary of what they were sending in the letter in hopes that whoever inspected the letters would not be tempted to keep the items. The military controlled Brazil, and almost everything coming into Brazil faced careful scrutiny. It usually took eight days to get a letter from the States, and while in Belem, the Redemptorist Fathers had a covert agreement with the airlines in which the mail bypassed the regular post office and went directly to the US to get mailed. Thus the constant pleas for American stamps and this agreement would cease affecting me when I was to go upriver.

Homesickness had been a very big issue for me for I had been experiencing vivid dreams of doing something with various family members. They were so vivid, and almost all the dreams were about scenes at home on the farm. In every one, toward the end, I tried to interact with someone, but he doesn't hear me. The characters continued to do what they were doing in my dreams. I felt as if I were watching them from some distant sideline, unable to communicate. Often, I would awake during these dreams and be very frustrated. Sometimes when I awoke in the mornings, I'd really need to force myself to shake off the loneliness, accept the fact of where I was, and remember why I had come to Brazil.

Letter to My Brother Bob
November 18, 1964

Hello, Brother Bob. Be sure to take care of my dog Duke, and make sure he's chained up to the doghouse every night so he doesn't wander. Make sure he is getting fed and watered daily. I know you are already taking care of all of that, but I had to write it anyway to make me feel better. I love and miss you all. Love, Marvin

Letter to My Twin Brother, Darwin
November 20, 1964

Greetings to my favorite twin brother. Be sure to give my hello to everyone. It was good to finally get a letter from home, and I feel so much better knowing that all is well. On our shortwave radio, the Papal Volunteers picked up the Notre Dame/Iowa football game, and everyone was cheering for Notre Dame so I started to cheer for the other side. The group had no idea that I had little interest or knowledge about sports. Halfway through the radio broadcast, I got up and went to my room to write letters and read. When I came back down, the group was afraid to tell me the final score of twenty-eight to zero. Iowa lost. I tried to tell everyone that I wasn't interested in sports, but they weren't buying it. During the time I was listening, the announcer said it was twelve degrees, and I had visions of the cold with snow blowing all over. This vision reappeared in my dream that night. I dreamt of snow blowing and covering everything and gradually covering the old Chevy (the Tank). My dog Duke had snow all over his face. The next night, I dreamt the same scene with the snow blowing, and I saw Joseph going into the hog house. I called out to him, and he just kept walking enough, even though he was very close to me and didn't hear me. Then I saw my brother Bob pushing through the snowdrifts, carrying a bale of straw. He also wouldn't even turn around when I called. Then I saw you, Darwin, trying to start your car, which refused to start. Strangely, I was standing by the pole in the yard with a bright light on top, and I couldn't move. No one saw me or would answer my calls. With that, I awoke all covered in sweat. I awoke with the feeling of being very cold, but instead it was very hot and humid where I lay. It

29

> *took me a minute to realize that I again experienced a very vivid dream. When I told other Papal Volunteers about my dreams, they all agreed they are experiencing more dreams, and some of them were just as wild as mine are. Give everyone my love. Love, Marvin*

My brother Bob had written me about pheasant hunting, and it made me hungry just to think of eating fowl. The only chicken we had to eat were very small morsels in the soup. I wrote home, "The chickens that Madre Ventura brings home alive from the market appear to be in such tough shape that the cooking staff at the house are doing these chickens a favor when they wring their necks."

I was due for a haircut about that time, and I went out at noon to get one. It was a mistake because every barbershop was closed for siesta from noon to three, as it was usually the hottest part of the day. I felt disappointed because I had a dental appointment at three o'clock that same day.

One of the student sisters said, "I'll cut your hair. I do it for all the sisters."

I was pressed for time so I agreed and sat down. I started to daydream while the sister toiled away. Within ten minutes, the sister said, "All done."

And it was the fastest haircut I ever had received. I went upstairs and looked into the mirror. I almost screamed out. I stared at myself in total disbelief for I couldn't believe that my mutilated head stared back at me in the mirror. I felt sick to my stomach. It looked as if the good sister had used a bowl on top of my head, and I knew for a fact that she hadn't. Word spread like wildfire throughout the school as I walked back downstairs stunned. As I descended downstairs, fifteen fellow students, laughing hysterically, stood there. I bolted back to my room and waited until it was time for my dentist appointment. Right after the dentist, I entered a barbershop.

The barber stared at the top of my head and muttered, "*Muito mal!*"[5]

As I sat in the barber chair while the barber attempted to salvage the situation, I pondered what some of the hair on those fellow nuns must have looked like.

At least they have their veils to hide their disasters.

---

[5] Very bad

Letter to Home
November 23, 1964

Dear all, Happy Thanksgiving to all, and it's wonderful to hear from home. Every day when the mail comes in, all of us here at Casa Central gather and watch everyone's reaction on what he is reading. Of course, none of us can wait to get to our room to reread our letters for we would rip them open right away and do a quick read. We save the rereading for the privacy of our rooms. When someone doesn't get a letter, all carefully note the reaction as well. I'm starved for information from home, and everyone breathed a sigh of relief when this letter arrived from you. John still hasn't received any letters at all, and I feel bad for him. But he acted as if it were nothing because he was used to it from being in the service. Another person, a nun and student at Casa Central, hasn't gotten any mail for two months. She finally got a letter today, and she nearly tore the letter in half trying to get it opened. Today is Thanksgiving Day, and I am writing this instead of eating supper. The reason is obvious for I am still stuffed. We all enjoyed a huge turkey dinner surrounded with beans, mashed potatoes, fresh-out-of-the-oven hot buns (which were out of this world), and huge amounts of fresh fruit. The buns reminded me of Mom's homemade bread, and then we proceeded to devour a very poor imitation of Mom's pumpkin pie. A lifelong dream was realized that day. At Mass at six in the morning, I got to serve as an altar boy. My heart was fluttering as I approached the chapel, and when I stepped into the chapel and genuflected instead of getting into a pew, I walked boldly to the sanctuary. When I entered, Father John turned and said, "Happy Thanksgiving. Are you ready?" I returned the greeting as I preceded the father to the altar. I could hardly contain my emotions because I was soon to serve my first Mass. I was so worried I would goof up, but the whole beautiful Mass went off without a hitch on my part. This is really Thanksgiving for me. After Mass, the whole group congratulated me, and I could tell they were all very happy for me. Some complained, however, that they were distracted with the thought I would goof up. Some said they were distracted about my haircut, especially their view of the back of my head. I can hardly believe the short time I have been on Brazilian soil. Despite the busy schedule, I'm so homesick. It must be because this has been my first Thanksgiving away from home. I am sending my love to everyone. Love, Marvin

Right after Thanksgiving, all the students from Casa Central motored two hours upriver via a very fast boat to an island in the Amazon. The island was small with white, sandy beaches. The locals advised us not to swim in the water due to the piranha. We totally ignored them because someone from the United States had said that piranhas do not swim in semi-salty water. This water was semi-salty due to the close proximity of the Atlantic Ocean. That advice sounded reasonable to us, so we all enjoyed the warm waters of the Amazon.

While in the kitchen that evening during meal preparation, in walked an old sow pig that resided at the nearest neighbor. I was standing in the kitchen, and I suddenly heard this familiar sound that took me back to our hog farm in Iowa.

I said to myself, "I can't believe what I'm hearing."

As I turned around, I saw this skinny, black, mangy, muddy, and stinking old sow groping for food. About half of the nuns present piled out of the house to get away from the creature; the other half of the nuns tried to chase it away. I suspected the brave nuns who stayed had farming in their backgrounds. The pig wouldn't budge so everyone started throwing it scraps, and in effect, the pig was rewarded for its intrusion.

The first night on the island, Ann was sleeping in a hammock outside on the front porch. At about two in the morning, she awoke to see what she thought what looked like a snake hanging from a low-hanging branch of a nearby tree. Ann let out this bloodcurdling scream, and we jumped out of our hammocks, which wasn't easy without hurting oneself. Most of us landed in a heap on the floor. We scrambling back to our feet; some of us stumbled around, trying to find out what was the matter. Others joined in the screaming contest. But the person sleeping in a hammock, about three feet above Ann, had draped her leg over the edge of her hammock in an attempt to stay cool, making a perfect image of a large snake's head in the dim moonlight. It took a while to get everyone settled down to very restless sleep. Everyone from school was along, and we spent two nights on the island. We returned the next day, tired, starving, stiff, sore, sun burnt, and happy.

ooked twice. They're
. The name refried beans
refritos, the Mexican-
anslated, *frijoles* means
os means "very (or well)
exican-Spanish, the prefix
indicate a repeated

Ⓜ | WORKMAN PUBLISHING

to My Brother Joseph
November 24, 1964

*etter finds everyone one well as I am here. John
novie being shown in the local theater. It was an
such a poor film that I have forgotten the title.
ear approached John and me, and he put on a
he terrible death that his mother was allegedly
n Portuguese, I told him I had no money. The
nd retorted, "My friend, you had money to go to
smoking and had a full pack of cigarettes. "You
n't you?" The beggar then went into this long
amaritan had pushed the pack into his pocket
t the man's feelings. After hearing all of that,
he beggar then asked, "Why?" I said, "Because
o my surprise, the man broadly grinned, shook
way laughing loudly. I remember one beggar
cut off at the elbows, and both of his legs were
ood in the center of the sidewalk, gripping this
. To me, it looked as if he were growing right
our of the sidewalk. I would guess he was in his early thirties, and I always
had something to give to poor fellows like him. So many beggars are on the
well-traveled sidewalks, and I see so many are crippled and deformed. I
guess that most of these deformities could have been prevented with early
intervention when these people were babies. Give everyone my love, and
please write again soon. Love, Marvin*

Some beggars would clog some of the busiest of thoroughfares and
try to bilk the passersby. On one occasion, this supposedly blind person,
with his eyes pinched tightly shut, was crying out very loudly for his need
of alms. As I passed, I dropped a heavy coin in his cup. After a few steps,
I turned to see the beggar reach into the cup and pull out the coin to
examine it with his eyes opened.

I would see a woman who looked in good health with a clean blanket
spread out onto the street, dressing and undressing a healthy baby while
she begged for alms. Another time, as I was passing a beggar, he rattled
his cup. I looked into the cup and spied this very unusual coin. So in

my broken Portuguese, I negotiated a trade. When I handed him the equivalent of a dollar for the coin, I reached in and took the coin I wanted. The beggar was lame but not blind, and he let out a wail of being robbed. I quickly dropped the coin back into his cup and fled the scene.

One particular day, I was standing in a long line to board a bus that would take me across town to the Redemptorist Fathers' main parish of Our Lady of Perpetual Help. This bus route was especially long because there always was a special adoration of the Virgin Mary on Fridays. I noticed how this one beggar used his hand that leprosy appeared to have ravaged. He would stand in front of a person, mumble about his affliction, and gradually bring his hand closer to the person. It usually worked because no one wanted a leper to touch him, so the person produced some kind of coin. When the man got to me, I was ready and dropped in a good amount.

The man worked the line as I thought, *Where is that bus?*

The bus was later than usual so the man started back down the long line, and many contributed again. When he came to me, I refused to give any more. As the beggar brought his hand up to my face, I didn't move. He looked me in the eye and hesitated with his hand barely touching my cheek. I could smell the rotting flesh as I calmly told the beggar I had already been generous and I would give no more. He stared at me for a second, but he put his hand down, walked to the end of the long line, and waited for the bus with the rest of us.

To my dismay, when I was ready to return to Casa Central on the bus, the same beggar was standing and working the line again from that side of town. I suddenly remembered I forgot something back at the fathers' house and I was no longer in a hurry. I decided I would ride later when the lines were shorter and the beggar was gone. I knew how he worked, and I didn't want to be a part of that again. This particular beggar only worked on the busy Fridays of the adoration times, and I knew I could avoid him by just being patient.

Transportation for the Papal Volunteers included walking to our destination, but if it were very far, one would have to resort to the very dilapidated bus system. It wasn't unusual for a bus designed to carry thirty passengers to be often crammed with sixty people or more. There seldom was a place to sit down, leaving one to hang on to the chrome bar above one's head. Often with the temperature hovering in the nineties most times, the armpit next to me was usually lethal, but it didn't seem to bother the locals at all to have a body partially pressed against each other. It was as if the bus driver wanted to fill his bus so full that it would be impossible for a person to fall down when he took the corners too wildly. For Americans, this was difficult to get used to, but the price of walking wasn't without its perils as well. Due to the very narrow cobblestone streets, buses often came way too fast to stop. They often jumped the curb and came up on the sidewalk with one set of wheels on the walkway to avoid a collision. Despite this, it was safe to walk at all hours of the day or night because muggings were unheard of in those days.

On the main thoroughfare of Belem, there were a few scattered stop-and-go lights but none on the side streets. This process regulated driving. The first driver to enter the intersection would only have to honk his horn first to be the one who was granted the right of way with his automobile. This regulation was null and void, however, when a bus would come barreling through. Everyone gave the buses a wide berth.

<hr />

My first impression of Belem was rapidly changing for the better. The first time I stepped out into the streets, I vowed I was going to write a book about Brazil. I marveled at the pitch-black, barefooted charcoal vendors who were covered in soot so thoroughly that one could only discern a smile and eyes. They went door to door with burlap sacks attached to their heads, leaving their hands free to do business. Many kitchens used charcoal on small hibachi-like stoves to heat water or cook small pots. With curiosity, I watched the deliverymen, also barefoot, carrying heavy loads on their heads, usually on the run throughout their route. Then there were the jockeys of horse-drawn carts with their thin and tired-looking horses or mules, en route somewhere to make *cruzerios*. The drivers usually mirrored the beast's disposition. All this was going on with traffic snarled everywhere for no driver was willing to yield the right of way. The loudest horn or most daring drivers helped sort out the question of right of way. Fire trucks, police, ambulances, and all buses were the exception to the rule because everyone knew their brakes were usually bad and they would have no problem running over the cars or people.

On one occasion, I borrowed the Redemptorist Fathers' Lambretta, a scooter-type vehicle, and headed off to Casa Central. I came to a busy intersection, stopped, and looked both ways, watching for buses, trucks, and cars. I saw none so I proceeded into the intersection. Lo and behold, a horse-drawn milk wagon pulled out in front of me. I could only lay the scooter on its side. I slid all the way under the cart, Lambretta and all. It was a good thing the horse had better brakes than most of the buses. The cart driver helped pull the scooter out from under the cart as traffic started to snarl and dozens of horns started honking. The only thing hurt besides my pride was the little horn button that was bent on the scooter and the tear in a brand-new pair of jeans that my mom had sent me. I was devastated for denim jeans were almost irreplaceable in Brazil. When I got the scooter back to the fathers, they weren't very happy and thus began a new policy that no one could borrow the scooter ever again.

Of all the employees at Casa Central, one particular fellow was Raimundo, a wisp of a man weighing less than a hundred pounds with coal black eyes that flashed with mischief. He was a custodian and helper around Casa Central. He had a real sense of humor, and it wasn't long before we were partners in fun-making. Even though Raimundo was in his forties, he loved a good prank. One particular day, I was on the second floor overlooking the walkway below. I was armed with a bucket of water, hoping to douse Raimundo good because he'd try to do that to me. As the shadow approached below, I dumped the bucket with full force. To my horror, the very tall person below was dressed in white, and it clearly wasn't Raimundo. There was no way I could recall the water back into the bucket, and I watched the water soak Madre Ventura's veil and habit from head to toe.

She looked up at my horrified frozen figure. "Come down here and explain what you are thinking."

I had to do some tall talking with many heavy apologies and a promise to settle down immediately and do whatever chore she would saddle me with. Raimundo loved it, and he laughed for days as I plotted to figure out another way to get him good. Before I left Casa Central, Raimundo crafted me a miniature wooden wheelbarrow, beautifully painted, which I proudly displayed on my dresser in my room.

It was about December 1 when I started to dream in Portuguese, and our teachers informed us that was a must if we were going to progress in the language. We were told we must stop converting English words into Portuguese. Instead, we must see the object or recognize the word in Portuguese. My other wild and frustrating dreams were also on the decline.

On one occasion while walking the streets of Belem, I purchased some chocolate squares. After getting back to Casa Central, I stashed the remaining other half in a tight-fitting tin. From day to day, I would reach into the tin and, without looking, pop a piece into my mouth. This one particular morning, however, after eating a few pieces, for some reason, I examined the next piece carefully before popping into my mouth. Very small, almost clear, beautiful red ants covered the piece in my hand. I couldn't help but wonder if eating ants were like eating earthworms, being 100 percent protein. I told myself to include in a letter home that, instead of eating chocolate-covered ants, I was eating ant-covered chocolates.

The humidity remained constantly high being on the equator. One day, I opened the closet in my room to check on my clothes stored there. Tiny brown eggs covered my suit, and I was informed it was necessary to send them out to the cleaners. It cost eighty-five cents to do the jacket and two pair of pants. The cleaners did a very nice job. My black dress shoes were a different matter for pure white mold covered them. All of my polishing wouldn't remove the white blotches on the shoes.

———

The local bishop of our diocese conducted class one day instead of our teacher, and he explained that, in 1952, the local money called the *cruzerios* was valued at par with the American dollar. Today in 1964, it took sixteen hundred *cruzerios* to buy a dollar. This happened mainly when the Brazilian government got the bill for the new modern city of Brasilia, and the government just printed the money to pay the enormous debt. The military ruled and controlled the current government, and according to the bishop, this government hadn't printed a single *cruzerio* and seemed determined to stay on course to stabilize the system. To aid the local economy, every imported item was taxed at 25 percent.

Letter to Home
December 6, 1964

Hello to everyone. Please keep the letters coming because it sure was good to get mail on this particular occasion. It was my turn to help with the dishes, and while I was doing so, I fantasized what was in the three letters that had just arrived. I admit I had a feeling of foreboding and apprehension. When I finally got done with dishes, I went to my room where I chose which letter to open first by the postmark of November 28. I could feel myself relaxing and the inner fears ebbing away until I hit the line, "Your brother Bob put a rope around his neck today." I tensed up again as my brain was flooded with terrible fears, and you wouldn't believe the horrific scenes that accompanied these thoughts as I almost fainted. I was so relieved to learn that you meant that he got engaged to marry instead of what first flew though my head. I felt a little foolish in letting my fears escalate so, and in so doing, I made a mental note to pray for Grandpa, who I knew was in the hospital, as I opened the November 30 letter. I started reading the second letter from you, and I was stunned. I couldn't let myself believe that Grandpa was dead. Mother, you apologized for the letter being short, and thank God it was for I was crying by the end of it. I had this lump in my throat that was so large that it felt like it was going to strangle me. I couldn't think a rational thought. I felt terrified and so alone. I didn't have my wonderful brothers and sisters here to seek comfort from. I got up from my chair in my room, went out into the streets of Belem, and walked. The streets were dark except an occasional streetlight, which I tried to avoid because I didn't want anyone to see the tears flooding out of me. How long I walked, I don't know, but it was a long time until I simply ran out of tears and I felt like I had a ton of bricks on my shoulders. When I got back to Casa Central, the local bishop was there, ready to take all the students to the art museum. When asked if I were going, I refused and went up to my room. Everyone just assumed I was still under the weather from being ill recently. After a while, Madre Ventura came to the room to check on me. When I told her what was wrong, she put her arm around my shoulder and said, "Oh, your grandfather is in heaven, and that is nothing to weep about." As she said this, I could see a mist clouding her glasses. I realized right there how blessed I was to be comforted by such a wonderful person. I made a vow to myself right then and there to never forget this moment. I spent two hours in the chapel Friday night, and during that, I did as you suggested and prayed to Grandpa. Then I prayed for the strength to carry on just as he did when he came to the United States as an immigrant. I recalled the tales of hardship he endured learning the English language, losing three different farms during the Depression, and the living through the three-year drought where he and his family lost everything. Above all, I prayed for the strength for Grandma to go on without Grandpa. I then arranged to have a special Mass offered in the chapel in honor of my wonderful grandpa. A feeling of love surrounded me at that Mass Saturday morning for everyone was there from Casa Central. My love to everyone, Marvin

The next day, I did one of the hardest things so far in my life, writing a letter to my grandma. I spent at least three hours, and it wasn't what I wanted to say yet. To my dearest grandmother, it was so hard to put deep-felt love into words. We only had our faith to help us believe that Grandpa was going to be okay, and that was what I wrote to her.

That following Thursday, a Papal Volunteer from Kansas named John, who was working at the Catholic hospital here in Belem, offered me the chance to ride along and visit a Japanese chicken farm. He was going to purchase some chickens for food for the hospital, and I accepted despite the fact I had to skip a class. We traveled in a VW Combie, and he could really maneuver through the crowded streets. When we got out of town, we flew down the roads at death-defying speeds of at least forty miles per hour. That was fast due to the roughness of the road surface and the winding nature of the road through the jungle. The driver had to be cautious of unexpected intersections, which had no yield or stop signs, and to take care if some animal or person just stepped out of the dense jungle foliage and into the road. For the most part, I had no idea where we were or what direction we were headed. Suddenly, we came upon this small clearing off the road. The first glance revealed a house made of cement that various pieces of junk, including weeds, surrounded. I couldn't help but marvel on how pretty the Japanese lady was who came to greet us, but her ill-fitting, tattered, and ragged-looking clothes were a distraction to her beauty. As John haggled about the price of the chickens, I looked around the complex. I was amazed at the long pole sheds, three in number, each about two hundred feet long. The sheds were packed with cages all in a long line that lined up the length of the sheds. Outside of the cages ran a long, narrow tray, just the right height for chickens. The tray contained clean drinking water for the chickens. Just below that was a food tray that also ran the whole length of the building. A small opening was in the cage, just enough for the caged chickens to poke their heads through to feed. The floor of the cage, where the hens stayed, was slightly sloped so when an egg was laid, the egg gently rolled safely into another tray below the feed tray, out of the hens' reaches. I was amazed to realize that one could care for these chickens totally without having to open the cage. There were two decks of cages and four rows of cages in each building.

One shed housed young hens ready to start laying eggs; the second shed was for the adult hens in full production of eggs; the third shed was for the old hens that were being sold for butchering. That was where we ended up to make our purchase at about a dollar each for a chicken. Just seeing the site gave me some ideas about chicken farming.

We returned to the cement building, where the eggs were hatched. From there, the hens began their journey. Along with the hatchery in the same building was a small grinder that ground the feed for the chickens. The cement building also provided housing for the family that owned and operated this enterprise. More amazing, several ducks, two dogs, and a few stray chickens shared the house. I was surprised to learn that this family was wealthy and had investments in several companies and two hotels, so this type of living was a choice they made. Most of the Japanese who set up small businesses such as this worked and saved with the ultimate goal of returning to their native country. But that plan usually ran amuck when their children considered Brazil as their home and didn't want to go to Japan.

Writing letters home and to other people consumed a lot of my spare time. In every letter, I did always have the same barrage of questions: How is the family? How is the old Chevy? How is Duke? How are the crops? How is the livestock doing? What is the weather like?

Letter to Home
December 10, 1964

Hello, everyone. It has been a week since I have received any letters, and just to mention that usually brings some letters in. To help us learn and to test our Portuguese, the students here in Casa Central put on six different plays tonight. The entire skit had to be in Portuguese, and I was in two. The skits went off really well, and everyone just loved them. I hope it helps to get everyone into the Christmas spirit because it sure doesn't seem like the season. All the Papal Volunteers are planning a big party after Midnight Mass, especially those around working in the city. Everyone is invited, no matter where it is going to be held. All the student nuns are practicing Christmas carols in Portuguese, and it seems so weird to hear familiar songs with a different language. In this letter, I'm sending some precious Brazilian stamps. I say precious because the people love everything about John F. Kennedy, and enclosed is the latest stamp in his honor. I put the stamps in the letter because people would steal the stamp right off the envelope due to everyone's love for him. It sure is settling for me to learn that everyone is well and most of my letters are getting to you. You have no idea how good it is to hear from all of you. Love, Marvin

On December 13, I rode all the way across town to go to the zoo, but when I got there, a big sign in English, German, and Portuguese stated, "Closed for the afternoon." So instead of just going straight back home, I decided to walk back home by traversing other various streets. I knew the general direction, and I took pictures as I progressed. On the way, I encountered a twenty-five-story apartment building.

Wouldn't it be grand if I could go all the way to the top and look out over the city?

I boldly walked right up to the elevator and pushed the button to the highest level, which was eighteen floors, and it worked. Once I climbed the remaining stairs to the very top, I was amazed that such a fine living area was intermixed with slum shacks, places of squalor, and nice homes. Obviously, little or no zoning regulations were enforced in Belem.

When I walked back home carrying my camera, I was the perfect mark for all the beggars in the surrounding area. As I rounded one of the corners on another street, one beggar came up to me, gripped my

41

hand, and started shaking my hand vigorously. This particular beggar was a rather repulsive fellow because festering sores covered his hands and scabs were everywhere on his body. This beggar was especially persistent and asked several times and in several different ways for money. When I told him I had none, the beggar grabbed my arm and pulled me to a nearby vending stand. I went along with his wishes, even though I didn't like idea of this fellow putting his hands on me. Then the beggar got aggressive and demanded money. He started to pull harder on me and toward the same street stand. Just then out of nowhere came this man who sternly commanded the beggar to let go. When the beggar complied, I stammered the words for "good night" in Portuguese, even though it was only three in the afternoon. I made tracks to the nearest washbasin and scrubbed my hands vigorously to rid myself of any possible disease. Most beggars weren't that aggressive.

On the way back, I stopped at a gift/smoke shop. Hanging there was a well-tanned alligator skin. It was over six feet long and over two feet wide. The tag on it was for fifty thousand *cruzerios* or about thirty-two dollars. I really wanted that one, and just as I walked out of the shop, someone bought it. One of the teachers from Casa Central said we shouldn't buy anything here in Belem because it should be cheaper in Coari where I was going.

Beggars were everywhere. One particular beggar stood by the very long line at the bus stop where I wanted to board. The beggar was shouting at everyone to give him money. Most people only had a few *cruzerios* to give, which he grudgingly accepted until he got to me. The smallest change I had was a bill for one hundred *cruzerios*, so not to get yelled at, I gave it to him. Rather than yell at me, the beggar turned on his heel, marched back to the end of the line, and held the bill above his head. The beggar was yelling that they could have done better in their giving. This beggar was a professional, and he allegedly made more than a construction worker did in a day.

On several occasions, families from the United States tried to conceal articles that were hard to find in Brazil in the mail. One particular family did get some through by sending a box of candy with each piece of film wrapped in tin foil instead of chocolates. That was very clever indeed. On another occasion, one of the nuns from Casa Central went to the post office to retrieve a magazine sent from the United States. Film was hidden in the rolled-up magazine. Customs was holding the magazine, and when the nun came to claim it, she was informed that she was going to be arrested. However, when the officials saw it was a nun, nothing was done, and the postal employee handed over the magazine.

> ## Letter to My Twin Brother, Darwin
> ### December 14, 1964
>
> *Hello to my favorite twin brother. Today I got wind that there could be plans for me to spend a month or so on a farm in Santarem. A Franciscan brother, who had once visited the farm operated by the Holy Cross Brothers, heard of my plans to farm in Coari and insisted I stop there on the way. Only time will tell if I'm going or not. On December 15, we are throwing an all-night party for two Papal Volunteer women who have completed their third year of commitment and were returning to the United States. All the Papal Volunteers seem to love parties, and any excuse would do. All of us here at Casa Central were invited to another party on last Saturday at the Hospital of Our Lady of Guadalupe to honor these same two Papal Volunteers. Best dress was required because the doctors at the hospital were hosting it. That meant I was to wear my suit I brought from the States. To my dismay, when I put on my pants, I couldn't believe how much weight I had lost. Everyone was waiting downstairs so I just hitched my belt two notches tighter and hurried off. When I finally got to a scale, I found I had lost quite a few pounds. I have been eating like a starved horse and still have lost weight, mainly from the waist and rear end. Keep writing. Love, Marvin*

Christmas was near, but it was especially hard to get into the Christmas spirit with the high temperatures and ever-present humidity. As there was no snow, Christmas trees, or usual Christmas decorations to bring the Christmas spirit, we had to rely mostly on the memories of our homes in the United States to get us in the mood.

Letter to My Younger Sister, Mary Jo
December 16, 1964

Hello, Mary Jo. How is my little sis doing? It sure was great getting a wonderful letter from you, and I can see the impish smile on your face. I shared your letter with several other volunteers, and when I showed Madre Ventura some of the pictures you sent, she started to sift through them with a broad smile on her face, as if they would bring back memories of her own way back in the days when she lived in Kansas. When she came to the picture of all of us, the one of all of us sitting in the living room, Madre exclaimed, "Oh, what a beautiful mother you have!" I noted tears in her eyes. I almost fell over for I hadn't expected a comment like that. In fact, I expected anything but that simple, beautiful heartfelt phrase. Suddenly, I felt ten feet tall. Oh, how right Madre is. We are very lucky for all of the wonderful memories I have of growing up and the wonderful childhood my parents provided for me. If I were to try to summarize my life at home, I would have to resort to the word "love." But even that word, which says so much, seems inadequate, especially with the holy season of Christmas in our midst. Oh, how many times I must have hurt my parents' feelings, but both of them accepted it as an expression of my love for them. Many a time since I have been away from home, I have knelt down in the chapel and thanked God for the privilege of being able to say, "They are my parents!" Keep the letters coming, and I am sending my love to you. Love, Marvin

---

On the equator, the sun was up by six every day. By nine, it was very hot, and everyone was sweating profusely by noon. By two, the clouds would roll in. By three, it would be raining really hard for about twenty minutes, and then the rain would stop suddenly. Within a half hour, the sun would be out again, and it would get hot and really steamy. A few exceptions to this weather pattern would be during the rainy season in which it would rain more and for a longer period of time.

About that time, Father Clemente took me out of class to discuss John's behavior. He informed me that John had proposed marriage to Ann, and it was causing a major problem for Ann. The father said that Ann had reported John's actions as stalking. This put me in a bad spot for I was John's roommate and I considered Ann a friend.

Letter to Home
December 20, 1964

Christmas greetings to everyone! Christmas sure sneaked up on me this year. I finally realized how close Christmas is because we put up a Christmas tree and other Christmas decorations today. We used a small tree from the jungle that only had bare branches, but the decorations helped make it look like a Christmas tree. While we decorated the tree, we played Christmas carols on the record player. We have lots of Christmas records, but they are never played during the rest of the year because hearing them makes everyone homesick. They sure are pretty, and they remind me of Christmas, but I'm going to miss the snow and all of my wonderful family. I'd like to send some gifts from here to home, but that's next to impossible. I was so surprised to get that package from home, even though I told everyone not to even try. Isn't that just like a mother to send something even when I advised her not to? I really enjoyed it though. I wish I was home to celebrate with you, but I will be home in three short years. Don't worry a minute about me for I'm so blessed with wonderful friends. We understand and love each other for we are all in the same boat. May the love and peace of the Christ Child dwell with you all of you. Love, Marvin

---

All of us really missed the dairy products from the United States. On a trip to the airport one week, some of the Papal Volunteers suggested we get an ice cream sundae from the local ice cream shop. Not being able to get ice cream anywhere, I agreed. It was the worst ice cream I had ever tasted, but it was so delicious. That was how desperate we were for ice cream. Apparently down here, they substituted fruit filling for dairy products. I didn't think I could ever get used to that.

About that same time, I got the official word that I would be going to Santarem for a month to learn from a Holy Cross Brother who had a farm there. This brother was reputed to be an ace farmer.

For something to do, I went along with Father Clemente to the post office one day to pass the time. When we got to the desk, I noticed a box with the symbols of poker chips and, to my dismay, my name on it. Father Clemente said I wouldn't be able to claim it until the post office sent me a slip. When I got back to Casa Central, I told Raimundo, who usually got the mail, to get a request slip. Perhaps he could claim the package while he was there that afternoon.

While eating supper that night with the other volunteers, Raimundo came in with the mail. Everyone except me bounded over to see what was there. Several people shouted that the package was for me, and they waited for my reaction, knowing how I usually reacted when the mail would arrive.

I just sat there calmly and continued eating. I responded with a simple, "Oh."

Everyone was dumbfounded with my reaction. I enjoyed the fact that I got them good. Everything in the package brought tears to my eyes as I found myself missing everyone at home so much.

One of the packages from home that made it through customs was a bottle of high-potency vitamin pills that my oldest sister, Marjorie, and her husband, a doctor, sent to me. I started taking them, and about the same time, I started getting severe boils on my neck, like I did while I was in high school. I stopped taking them, thinking they caused my boils and large pimples. I had no clue that this was the beginning of my onset of type II diabetes. I didn't learn this as a fact for years to come.

Letter to Home
December 28, 1964

Hello, everyone, and Christmas greetings to all. I sure have an empty feeling for not being home for Christmas, and I'm so glad you had a good Christmas. I did too, but I missed you all terribly. I have been told to be away the first Christmas is the hardest, and I sure hope so because this has been hell. Tomorrow I have a doctor's appointment to see the cause of my severe pimples and boils. It was really something to get a handwritten letter from you, Dad, and I feel very fortunate to get a letter expressly from you. I couldn't recall my dad ever writing a letter, and I felt special indeed. There is this priest at Hospital Guadeloupe, and he is suffering from what is believed to be spinal meningitis. This priest is suffering from seizures and hemorrhaging of the brain. I knew this because, when I was at the hospital on one occasion, I was asked to help hold him down for a spinal tap. His spinal tap was really difficult, and it would take a lot more people to hold me down than what it did for him, especially when I would see the size

---

of the needle. It was huge, and the nurses would insert that needle deep into the spinal column in his lower back to drain the fluid into a very large syringe to reduce the pressure on the brain. His spinal fluid had much less blood in it, which was a good sign, and he was then scheduled to leave for the United States the next morning because the hospital staff felt he would be safe to travel. I later learned he died in a hospital back in the United States. Love, Marvin

Despite this sad time, I continued to hit the streets with anybody who was game to go along with me. Ann and I traversed many a mile exploring the city, and we found solace in being able to talk about the events at home. Ann and I became good friends. She was there for me when I received word that my grandfather had died. I was there for her while John continued to stalk her. Apparently, John had developed a crush on her, and he wasn't very good at showing how he loved her. I couldn't believe it, but, sure enough, most every time when we went out of the door of Casa Central, John would follow us, staying back about one-half of a city block and continuing to spy on us. Shortly thereafter, I confronted John and told him that he was scaring Ann and he should leave her alone. John demanded I stay out of it and I stop being her friend.

After witnessing several occasions that frightened Ann, I went to Madre Ventura and Father Clemente. Things got worse before they got better, and John was finally asked to leave the Papal Volunteers program. The hopes for radio communication for the Redemptorist Fathers went back to the United States with John.

When John received word that he was being sent back to the United States, he first cried. Then he later seemed very relieved and finally thought the whole thing was funny. John had been under a terrific strain, trying to learn Portuguese and living with nuns, priests, and brothers. Considering his military background, that might have been the most difficult, along with having Ann around, whom he thought he was in love with.

Marvin J. Schuttloffel

Letter to Home
January 2, 1965

Merry Christmas a little late, but late is better than never. John is being sent home, and he has agreed to take some gifts back to the US to mail upon arrival to my family, provided I get them purchased, wrapped, and addressed right away. So here they are.

Dad: Here is a boa constrictor snakeskin, and may it drive out the evil spirits of the Farm Bureau.

Mom: Here is a silver spoon bearing the seal of Brazil. Also included is a red kerchief that ties in the back of your lovely head. May all your days be as bright as this kerchief.

Gerry: Here a letter opener to be used for all the letters you receive from me.

Linda: Here is another silver spoon for your precious collection, and allow me to add to it.

Joe: Here is some Brazilian money. Let it help pay for some joy to you.

Bob: Here is a cigarette case containing a pack of Brazilian cigarettes. The matches that are included are to replace the ones I stole from you.

Darwin: Here is a spider to scare all the girls away, and may it be very effective until I get back.

Mary Jo: Last but not least, here is a Brazilian flag. May it help you in advance in knowledge in any subject you take. Also included is a coin purse from Mexico, and may it always be full of money for you.

These are just a few souvenirs from Brazil, and even though they aren't much, it made me stop and realize that I could never send a gift that could repay what you all have done and are doing for me. Please enjoy, and I wish there could have been more. Merry Christmas a little late. Love Marvin

---

The other night when John was packing to go home, I sat in the same room and watched as he packed. I felt terrible about him going back home, and I wished I was going with him. But that feeling has now passed, and I'm glad it worked out like it did. John had the light on in our room as he packed into the night, so I decided to sleep in the sewing room down the hall. First, I had to find a hammock to string up, so I located an extra one. After hanging the hammock, I searched for a mosquito net. After being out of the room for twenty minutes or so, I came back to the sewing room empty-handed,

48

> *but as I entered the room, I noticed a net had already been hung up over the hammock. I thought of how nice it was for one of the nuns to help care for me, and I remember thinking, "It must have been Madre Ventura who is always thinking of me." With lights off, I climbed into the hammock and settled in for a rest. Just as I was about to doze off, I heard bare feet coming up the steps and down the hall. Someone was coming down the hall from the nuns' sleeping quarters. I lay perfectly still and listened intently. Her footsteps told me she was coming right into the sewing room where I lay. The door suddenly swung open, and this female creature, all ready for bed, walked right up the hammock and started to get in. Here I was lying in the hammock with just my underwear on as this poor unsuspecting nun tried to get in the hammock as well. I lay very still as if asleep for I wanted no screaming. Suddenly, this nun stiffened up and took off running down the hall and back downstairs. I stayed in the hammock, shaking like a leaf when about a dozen nuns came thundering up the stairs. One knocked on the door, demanding to know who was in there. I quickly confessed though the door by telling them in rapid succession of all the events that led me to this room. All the nuns were so relieved to hear it was I, I wasn't up to no good, and I did indeed have a valid reason to be in the sewing room. Realizing my embarrassment, the nuns told everyone, and by the next morning, I was famous. To make a long story short, I stayed in the sewing room that night, and the poor nun had to go somewhere else to sleep. Love, Marvin*

A few days after that incident, Madre Ventura approached me and said she could arrange for me to visit some of the local vegetable farms near Belem. Perhaps I could get an idea of what I was facing as far as farming in the Amazon. It sounded like a great idea, and Madre Ventura's friend whisked me away the next morning in his jeep. The driver and I traveled outside of the city for about five miles and stopped at several small plots of land that were cultivated with many different kinds of vegetables. People of Japanese descent manned them all. The whole family would come out to greet us and welcome us as distinguished guests. Language was a real issue as most of the adults spoke very little Portuguese, no English, and very good Japanese. I, in turn, spoke very little Portuguese, no Japanese, and very good English. The solution was simple. We both spoke to the children, and between my English and their Japanese, the children were able to unravel it all. I soon learned that, when I had trouble communicating, I would seek out some kids who, no matter what race they were, tuned into English.

One particular farm had hybrid chickens with raised hen coops, and my interest piqued. The farmer, wife, and children explained the reason for elevating the hen house, how they fed them, and the advantages of growing hybrid chickens for the hungry city. I learned a lot that day, and at that point, I had no idea how this day would affect my future success in Brazil.

———————

All of the Papal Volunteers were on a salary of seventy dollars a month. Forty of that was to go to housing and food, leaving roughly one dollar a day, which didn't go very far. There was much concern about inflation, and rumor alleged that prices were going to double again after the first of the year. It was said that the prices were in the control of the military government. These rumors became a reality right about the time they said it would, and it put a burden on everyone. The banks had very few small investors. With the realization of inflation, people immediately spent their wages on buying something that would hold its value before the prices would double again. A bottle of beer (something I could relate to) in Belem cost about fifty cents, but it contained a full liter, almost a quart of beer. Just to show how inflation was rising, when we arrived here two months before, beer was about thirty cents a bottle.

When walking through one of the many parks, mango fruit was falling very regularly. One about the size of large potato fell and struck me on the wrist. Man, did that hurt for several days. Being American, I didn't have enough sense to stay out of the parks when the mangos were falling. The locals knew better, and I'm sure they got a charge out of us silly foreigners. I vowed I would get even by eating one. It was the most difficult task for the fruit was so stringy and the strings would get stuck in one's front teeth.

I was going through that area to visit a co-op that two Papal Volunteers from Kansas ran. When I was looking at the operation, the two pleaded with me to come and help them run it for a while so they could return to the United States as their time was up and they didn't intend to stay longer. I declined to help for I knew that, if I agreed to stay a short while,

I would be stuck in Belem for the next three years and I would never get to Coari as I planned.

———

One day, Pat, a student volunteer from Illinois, came out of the kitchen, screaming her lungs out. "There's a huge spider on the wall!"

I took one glance and ran to get my camera. This spider stood two inches tall and was six to seven inches across. On his back was a brightly colored X. A thick tan and brown hair, which was about a quarter inch long, except for the bald area that displayed the X, covered the spider's back and whole body. This particular spider's bite was quite painful (I was told) but wasn't usually fatal.

Suddenly, Madre Ventura boldly walked in with a kitchen broom and took a swift swing at the spider clinging to the tiled kitchen wall. The first time, the spider jumped right at her, but the sister, being an old hand at this type of combat, was ready. As the spider sprang at her the second time, even though it jumped the length of the broom, the sister quickly stepped back. As she did, she took another swing with the trusty broom, knocking the spider to the floor. The spider had no recourse but to run for it. The next blow from her trusty weapon proved fatal for the spider, and the spider's speed was no match for the swiftness of her broom. As we gathered around the spider's corpse, we were told not to touch the spider because the hair could get embedded into our flesh due to the tiny barbs at the end of its hair. I was a lot more cautious about entering the kitchen after that.

Letter to My Little Sister, Mary Jo
January 16, 1965

Hello, Mary Jo. I'm so glad you received the Brazilian flag I sent you. You asked about the flag's significance. Although I cannot guarantee this information is factual, the green stands for the huge jungles and landforms. The yellow stands for the gold that is supposed to be found in the interior somewhere. The stars stand for the states of Brazil. I do not know what the white stands for, but the words "Ordem e Progresso" stands for "Order and

> *Progress." That is all about I know of the flag so far, but as I learn more, I will let you know. I met two Papal Volunteers who are in Belem vacationing upriver. One by the name of Ray is bunking with me since I have an extra bed in my room with John being gone. Ray is from Whittemore, Iowa, and seems like one heck of a nice guy. The exciting part is we will both be in Coari together. I know we will get along just fine, and I really like him. Keep those letters coming for I sure do treasure them. By the way, next time tell me about your boyfriends. Ha ha. Love, Marvin*

During Ray's stay, I gained a lot of insight about Coari and the happenings there, but despite all of our conversations, I couldn't picture clearly in my mind what it would be like there. Ray couldn't give me much help on the farming situation, and even though I wanted to glean more information out of him about life in Coari, I had to go to class, and Ray had people to see and errands to run. It wasn't long, and Ray was on his way back upriver.

One night, I was sitting right where I usually sat to write letters and to complete my homework. Out of the corner of my eye, I noticed a big, black bug lumbering toward me from the other side of the room. As this bug drew closer, it displayed no fear that I could see. I could see it had this very large snout and no wings. When he got by my chair, I dropped a small wooden box on him, and this bug, becoming furious, started to attack the box. I could hear this crunching noise as the bug bit into the wood. I realized this was no ordinary bug, and I didn't want a bug that was so strong to bite me. I grabbed one of my heavy boots and slammed it down on him. It took several hits of my boot to slow him down. To my surprise, when I showed the bug to Madre Ventura the next morning, she informed me that I had killed a scorpion.

On occasion, the staff at Casa Central would arrange for guest speakers to come to our classes and help us adapt. A German priest working in the Chingue River area, which savage tribes of native Indians still inhabited at that time, held one class. He showed me the slides with some beautiful slides of sunsets of the area, and I hoped I could get some great pictures like that. The poverty displayed there was sickening, and the life expectancy was deplorable. The priest showed slides of this one tribe that numbered over one thousand people. He had lived in their midst for eleven years before he became ill and was called back to Germany. When the same priest returned five years late, no one recognized him. No one knew him. All of the people he had known from before had died off, and a whole generation had passed in just five years.

Letter to Home
January 21, 1965

Hello to everyone in the US. Keep those awaited letters coming for it assures me that everything is okay there as it is here in Belem. Ray, the Papal Volunteer from Coari, is in the Hospital Guadalupe to rid himself of a few parasites. Though he appears to be healthy, I'm told he will be there for four days. I really get a bang out of this guy, and although he seems rather quiet, he can really get going. From his stories, I can tell Coari will be quite an experience, and I can't wait. Today Casa Central got a visit from a representative of the Health Ministry, and he took blood samples of all of us here. Apparently, there is a mosquito-borne disease called "elephantitis", and so far, over thirty-five thousand people here in Belem have been infected with it. Those who have it have their legs swell up so badly that you cannot tell where their knees or ankles are due to the severe swelling. This swelling never passes, and there is no cure. I saw several cases of people with it, but I never knew the cause or what it was called. You be assured that, from now on, I will make sure my mosquito netting will be closed extra tightly before retiring. I am enclosing lots of love. Love, Marvin

---

At one party, a Holy Cross Brother named Brother Ben made a gallon of punch, and half was rum. Brother Ben put in two fifths of rum, and all of the nuns at the party seemed to really like the taste. The nuns didn't get roaring drunk, but they sure got silly. The next morning, they looked like scrub mops, and I got a real bang out of seeing nuns with a hangover. I had seen many crazy things since being in Brazil, and this one would be among the top five.

Letter to My Brother Joseph
February 21, 1965

Hello, Joseph. It sure was good to hear from you, and don't let anybody tell you that you don't write a good letter. Reading it is the difficult part! (Just kidding.) I'm sending your birthday gift early because I may forget, and I heard today that my course in Portuguese would end February 27. I will be staying in Belem until March 4 or 5. At that time, I will be leaving Belem and heading for Santarem, where I will spend a month of intense training on farming in Brazil. As you already know, your birthday falls in March, but with my travels, it may be difficult to send something. I said I may forget, but I just said that to get your dandruff up. So here is a happy birthday wish, and I ache for the chance to be there with you to celebrate, but God has different plans. (I hope he know what he is doing!) Tomorrow night is the graduation parties for the five Canadian nuns who will be going to Fortaleza to open a new hospital there. I will surely miss this group, and I plan to vacation in Fortaleza and visit these nuns before I leave Brazil. Wednesday night, another Papal Volunteer and I, along with four nuns, had a graduation celebration, and I received my diploma. These diplomas hold no scholarly significance because we were the first class to make them up and they aren't worth the paper they're written on, but it will serve as a sweet memento of the wonderful time spent here at Casa Central. At any rate, getting them is a perfect opportunity to host a celebration bash. Write me more. Love, Marvin

---

Graduation day at Casa Central was on February 27, 1965, and shortly after the party, I planned to head upriver, happy the schooling process was over. Yet I knew I would miss the friends I made, and I refused to believe that I would never see some of them again. I knew it was time to go, and as I did, the little butterflies in my stomach took flight once more as I realized how much I missed my family back in the United States. I had tremendous fear for the unknown.

About that same time, Casa Central also received word that five more sisters from Canada would be arriving Tuesday, March 9. I believe these sisters were of the same order that was here before. They were all so nice, and these nuns were currently working in Fortaleza at the new hospital there.

When the first set of nuns left Casa Central, they gave me six padlocks, six flashlight batteries, a box of syringes, and needles, all of which I was sure would come in handy at the hospital in Coari.

I was supposed to depart several weeks earlier from Belem, but I had to wait for the trunk I had packed in Sioux City. It finally arrived, thanks to the good ship *The Del Monte*. I was able to go through it and sort out what belonged to John, who was now back in Milwaukee. I shipped back everything that was John's in his own trunk. My trunk was then to be sent all the way to Coari via the fathers' boats.

I was finally able to purchase my plane ticket for Santarem, and at last I knew for sure of my departure date and time, March 26, 1965, because I now had the tickets in my hand. The five-hundred-mile flight cost fifty dollars, which my future boss in Coari paid for. I knew I would be flying in a DC-3, and I heard they were reliable.

CHAPTER 5

ON THE FARM

SANTAREM, BRAZIL

I looked forward to going to Santarem to learn more about Brazilian farming, and I pondered what it would be like as I was flying over the Amazon River. Finally in the air, I found it amazing that, everywhere I looked, I saw great expanses of water and trees that looked like toys, but I knew the trees exceeded 150 to 200 feet in height. Every so often, I'd see a small clearing in the jungle where someone had built a house with a grass-thatched roof and was eking out a living by what he could glean from the jungle.

Just outside of Belem, we flew over immense amounts of marshlands as we followed the Amazon for about an hour. Then for the next two hours, the land appeared drier, and by the time we got to Santarem, sagebrush and dry land appeared to fill the land. The flight was wonderful, and I saw some beautiful sights as we flew over the countryside. The landing into Santarem was a bit rough after three hours of flying time.

As soon as I arrived, several secular priests and one American greeted me. We had lunch and then a short siesta. We then boarded a jeep and headed for the farm of the Holy Cross Brothers, about seven miles out into the country. The road was very rough, and some of the sand pockets were so deep that we almost tipped over twice. We spent the last two miles climbing this very steep grade, and it was quite a grind for the vehicle. When we reached the top of the very steep hill, I saw the most beautiful scene I had ever encountered. As I looked out over the edge of the hill, I could see out for miles, looking across two huge rivers, the Solomons and the Tapa Jose Rivers. The Tapa Jose was a beautiful, clear blue; the Solomons was this huge mass of brown, surging water. From my vantage point, I could see where the two rivers merged and water from the Tapa Jose gradually blended into the Solomons. Quite soon, the water had all turned this dirty brown, and it seemed the Tapa Jose was to be lost forever.

Brother Norbert said he was late for evening vespers prayer with the seminarians as he sprang from the jeep. Brother Norbert told me I should wait outside until I was summoned for evening meal. It was a beautiful dusk as the sun was setting in the tropics, and I wandered over to the edge of the hill to get a better view. When I looked over the valley below, I was astounded to see the very vista that had appeared to me many times in my childhood dreams. It was like déjà vu all over again. I felt I had been here before so many times, standing at this very edge of this vista. A warm, serene feeling enveloped me, and I knew right then and there that God wanted me to be there. For the first time in a long while, I felt confident and at peace with my commitment to the Papal Volunteers. I was convinced this was some sort of mini miracle in my life, and I never had a feeling like that before and never since then.

The location for the farm was chosen because the soil was beautiful black, loamy soil. Unfortunately, this good farming soil was only about four inches deep. Brother Norbert was well aware that extra care had to be taken to preserve this soil and not allow it to erode down the hill during tropical rains.

Brother Norbert's previous experience included being a lumberjack, and this really came in handy in helping clear roughly five hundred acres of the two-thousand-acre plot that the brothers owned. The brothers were primarily there to operate a junior seminary for boys, which was designed to prepare young candidates to decide if they should enter the seminary of the Brothers of the Holy Cross. The farm was located on a place called *Diamintino.*[6]

Brother Norbert was a very interesting man. I finally had met an American whose Portuguese was worse than mine was, and he had been in Brazil for ten years. Brother Norbert still could communicate with the natives of Brazil using a series of gestures and grunts. Amazingly enough,

---

[6]   Diamond Mountain

he ran what he called a volunteer trade school that trained volunteers from the local area in some of the basic skills of welding, plumbing, electrical work, blacksmithing, and auto mechanics. Just the simplest of skills would be very helpful to these young Brazilians in starting a trade for themselves when they returned to their native villages. In trade for this training, the volunteer students would assist in the duties of farming. People who knew Brother Norbert said he was a very quiet man until he could talk farming. Needless to say, he talked my ear off and would answer my questions in great detail. As we approached the seminary, he explained the name of Diamond Mountain. When the land was cleared, this huge area stood out so big and high in the horizon that the hill allegedly got so large because diamonds were underneath the surface. Brother Norbert laughed and said he wished it were true as we rounded the last curve to the top.

After evening meal, I met the other brothers and the twenty-some seminarians there. While the rest of them socialized, I was shown my stark room, located in a machine shed near the chapel. The room consisted of a hammock with mosquito netting draped over it and a chair. A small bathroom was in a small room adjacent to my hammock. Getting into the hammock required more skill than I realized, and after several attempts, I mastered the challenge. The main thing was to make sure there were no open gaps where the mosquito netting touched the floor. Also, the thin blanket was to be used under oneself when the cool jungle night set in, unlike how we used a blanket in the United States on top of us. When I awoke in the morning, several species of large insects were clinging to the netting, and thankfully, all were on the outside of the net.

My schedule here at Diamond Mountain went something like this. At five in the morning, Brother Norbert started the big diesel generator, and all the lights would come on. So everyone would get up, including me. After shaving and other duties, we would head for the chapel for five thirty Mass. Right after Mass, breakfast was served, and everyone was at his job by seven fifteen. At eleven forty-five, everyone went back to the chapel to give thanks for the day and the offering of our meal prayers. We are allowed ninety minutes to eat and take a quick nap. At one thirty, all work resumed and continued to five thirty when we all would again head back to the chapel to give thanks and say evening grace. Evening meal was served promptly at six, and immediately after, all could enjoy a card game or two. At eight sharp, a bell would summon everyone back to the chapel. After about twenty minutes of prayer, we all headed for our rooms, or we could continue our recreation. At nine thirty, Brother Norbert would shut off the generator, and all of the lights would fade out, as if in a theater. I'd either better be in bed or have a flashlight handy to help find my way for it got very dark. Within minutes of lights out, the jungle noises would start and last through the entire night, only to subside when the five o'clock bell shattered the din and daylight spread its orange glow.

Starting right off, after learning the above routine, I was informed that my first day would be spent assisting Brother Norbert in inoculating the herd of Brahma cattle that was pastured in the nearby jungle and some cleared patches of land. Every other day, we had to corral them and swab their four hoofs with a creosote-like substance to prevent a certain insect from laying its eggs on the cattle's heel. If the eggs were allowed to hatch, the larvae would enter the heel and cause the heel to itch. When the cow felt the itching, it tended to lick the heel to ease the itching, and that was how the eggs got into the cow's system. If the disease were left untreated, the cow would eventually develop a high fever and die.

The treatment included scrubbing the interior of the cow's mouth with a lemon and salt solution designed to heal any sores in the cow's mouth. These cows had been vaccinated for this disease about six months before, but the symptoms developed anyway. Just to be safe, we gave them another shot as a backup prevention.

These cattle were mean and very stubborn and didn't like being told what to do. They really didn't like the treatment we were using either. I learned very quickly that Brahma cattle can seldom be forced to do anything and they have a very stubborn streak. If they were roped around the horns, they simply went down on their knees and refused to budge. While in this stance, it would be foolhardy to approach them. Some of these animals weighed in excess of fifteen hundred pounds and would explode in pure rage when approached if being held by their horns. The only solution was to corral the cattle individually into a sturdy wooden stanchion, work through the side of the timbers, and never approach them from the top of the stall.

My job was to swab the heels, hooves, front legs, and around the horns with a disinfectant that was to destroy the eggs laid there. Finally, I was to inject the animal with an inoculation with a very large needle and syringe. I had to be very careful not to have the needle break off when the fifteen pounds of pure hell broke loose due to the injection. Neither part of the operation ever went smoothly because of the breed's fierce temper.

This process went on for several days because of the size of the herd and every animal had to be treated several times. Every animal seemed to have its own idea about the corral. Almost every one of the Brahma cattle had stains of blood on their necks indicating the spot where vampire bats had been the previous night. It looked as if the bats knew right where to hook on to the cow's neck to access the blood veins, and it was a spot that was difficult for the animal to scrape the bat off.

Another problem Brother Norbert faced was that his 350-pound boar pig had lost the power to stand up. The boar's hind legs were very weak. The brother and I spent about a half hour each day trying to get the boar pig to stand and develop some strength in standing. I surmised that this pig never would be able to function in the capacity it needed to. The brother arranged to get a replacement shipped in from the United States. This pig had sired many a pig for Brother Norbert, and he had about fifty really nice young shoats getting fat.

Some of the things that Brother must do to raise things down here just amaze me.

I next got involved with cutting cornstalks by hand and bringing them in from the field. Once there, we fed the stalks into a tractor-powered chopper that blew the shredded corn bits into a cement block ring in an attempt to make silage for the cattle. Although corn was a good choice for Brother Norbert to grow because of the amount of cattle and hogs he raised, I knew this type of farming was out of the question for me in Coari.

One night, I got careless about the placement of the mosquito netting around my hammock. Deep into the night, I felt something crawling up my right leg, about mid-calf. Not really waking up, I took my other foot and brushed it off my leg. Wham! I felt this unspeakable pain on my leg, and I quickly grabbed my flashlight to see what was going on. I only caught a glimpse of a hairy insect retreating under my hammock. I leaned out of the hammock to get a better look, and naturally, I was flipped right out of hammock onto the floor, pulling the net down around me. I never did get another look at whatever bit me. By the next day, my leg was swollen so tight and round that I couldn't tell where my knee or ankle was. There wasn't a lot of pain, and I could walk like a pirate. When I was asked what happened, I could only say a very hairy thing bit me. The swelling finally went down in five or six days. Brother Norbert told me I was lucky to be healthy as I was because some of the local people wouldn't have survived such a bite due to the condition of their livers from contracting hepatitis after drinking unfiltered water.

Fourteen boys were at the farm, and they were between the ages of sixteen and eighteen. All were in their various stages of candidacy for becoming a Brother of the Holy Cross. About twelve brothers were here to teach and assist the boys in their studies. Four of the twelve brothers actually lived at the farm where I was; the others lived in town at the school that the seminarians went to during the day.

The school was actually first built as a hospital that Henry Ford funded, but it failed to function. The brothers procured the building and converted it into a seminary and school that at least half of Santarem's youth attended as well. The seminarians were ferried back and forth for noon meal and evening stay in a flatbed Ford truck.

After two weeks of being there in Santarem, I had the opportunity to get quite an education. Brother Norbert was the perfect teacher, and I assumed he was about thirty-five or so. He had the patience of Job, and he was always planning new schemes to expand this, try that, or simply change something already tried. He reminded me of my brother Joseph, who was always planning and trying new things on the farm in Iowa.

As an example, while I was there, Brother Norbert was planning to clear more jungle, and he had an idea how to build a new corn sheller to shell corn that was raised here on the farm. He also planned to make a boat-powered grass chopper. During the dry season, people went out into the swamps by canoe and cut grass by using a hand machete. The process was very slow. The local farmers badly needed the grass to feed their small herds of cattle, especially the people who couldn't afford pastureland or the means to rent the land. The grass in the swamps was always tender, and there was no limit on the acres of grass available. It was impossible to let the cattle graze in the swamps because too many head of cattle were often lost to drowning, especially when the rainy season resumed.

The history of the farm was very interesting. Brother Norbert came to Santarem in 1958, and he had the backing of almost ten thousand dollars from a benefactor in the United States. The money contained the provision that it had to be used to purchase land for farming. The brothers were able to make a purchase of ten thousand acres, mostly jungle-covered and believed to be unable to be tilled. Brother Norbert started with a plan of clearing only twenty acres at a time. If one cleared too much, the jungle would just creep back in. All the trees felled to clear the land were piled up and burned. It was soon evident that the area of the burn pile was where the crops grew the best, pointing out the soil's lack of potash.

Brother Norbert used a German-made disc/plow for no plow could handle the many rigid tree roots. The first crops planted in the cleared fields were always corn. It was common to see the corn up within three days after being planted due to the high temperatures and bountiful rain. Little or no cultivating was needed the first year because the burning had destroyed all the weed seeds. In the second and third year, a through cultivating was needed. Despite all of that, the jungle would still creep back in. The cleared fields were allowed to have tree stumps left in the field, and after three years of crops, the field was abandoned, and the jungle was allowed back in. Five years later, the process would start all over again on the same field.

Brother Norbert deviated from this recycling process by planting a fast-growing grass called "elephant grass." The name was possibly due to the height of this grass because it grew higher than an elephant. The elephant grass was planted while the corn was nearly knee high. The grass would grow rapidly and spread its roots over the entire field. After the corn was handpicked, Brother Norbert would come in with his disc/plow and chop up the cornstalks and grass into small bits. All the little pieces of cut-up grass would take root and spread faster than the jungle could. Within six months after the corn was picked, the grass was ready to be pastured, and the cattle would gorge themselves on the tender elephant grass. The best part of the whole operation was the fact that the field stayed open for the grass prevented the jungle from taking over again. Erosion was less of a problem. But there was no way to stop the grass from spreading, and using the disc/plow only made it worse. The huge trees of the jungle often shadowed the edges of the field where the grass had been planted. The elephant grass required full sun to grow and thrive enough to prevent the jungle from creeping back in. This process would perpetuate itself, and the jungle would creep in as the band kept closing in on the fields. To prevent this, Brother Norbert would disc up that belt every few months, thus cutting the jungle invasions and replanting the elephant grass. If a field wasn't disced/plowed, it would lose about ten feet in circumference every year.

Letter to Home
April 12, 1965

Greetings to everyone from the farm in Santarem. Last week, I was struck down with what a doctor would call homesickness, and I'm sure that's what it was. I wasn't sick in bed or anything, but I sure missed home. I guess being out here farming just brought back too many good memories for it was the worst bout I've ever had since leaving home, but now I seem to be over it. The main thing that helped me recover was that I kept reminding myself that I had agreed on three years. I'm going to stick it out. The other thought that helped was that this stint is only for three years, and I must give credit to the Lord for answering my prayers. Today, I got a letter from Father Clemente, and he advised me that he would meet me in Manaus on April 24, and we would travel upriver from there, so it looks like I have twelve more days here on the farm in Santarem. The time spent here in Santarem was well worth it, and I consider Brother Norbert a saint. He has accomplished so much in six years, and he is a very patient teacher. Don't worry about me. I'm fine, and please remember that I pray for you all every day at Mass. Love, Marvin

---

Right after receiving word on the date and time I would be moving, Brother Norbert and I traveled to two different farms to look over their operations so I could get a different perspective on farming in Brazil. The farms we did visit couldn't compare to Brother Norbert's farm. One of the farms had a series of three poles forming a triangle stuck into the ground. Pepper vines clung to the posts. The crop didn't look too good because it seemed to be suffering from some insect infestation. The ground appeared to be very dry, and no irrigation was available. The other farm was trying to grow corn, but it also looked like the crop was in stress. I surmised the ground was lacking needed nutrients, which only made the crops do more poorly during the time of drought. None could compare to Brother Norbert's crops. Before returning, we visited the school where the brothers taught. All the kids seemed really nice, well behaved, and very proud to be a part of that school.

While I was at the school, I stood on an outside stoop, and a beautiful blue and yellow macaw was with me. This bird was very friendly, and it gestured to me to put out my hand so it could step onto it. Instead, I stuck my finger in its mouth to feel it's very fat tongue. One of the brothers grabbed my hand and cautioned that I could and probably would lose a finger in the process. The brother than picked up a Brazil nut and handed it to the macaw. With one foot, the large bird placed this thick-shelled nut into its beak and cracked it with ease. I was astounded and very grateful for the brother's intervention.

When we returned to the farm, Brother Norbert and I checked on the boar pig. He seemed to be stronger and could stand longer, but the boar had a very sore spine and would squeal when touched. One of the Brazilian workers said the pig had *mal de caldera.*[7] I learned the Brazilians would name anything literally by what they could see.

I learned that hybrid corn seed from the United States wouldn't grow well in Brazil. Brother Norbert had tried some, and he said the husk that covered the ear was too thin and tended to open when the weather was dry. The open ends of the ear allowed beetles to enter and destroy the corn inside the husk. Corn that had adapted to this climate had a much thicker husk and stayed tightly bound during the growing process. At least double the amount of foliage was on the cornstalk, which helped prevent the sunshine from reaching the jungle foliage creeping back in. This kind of hybrid corn was developed in Brazil by Brazilians and could work in Brazil. Some kind of a bug always seemed to be just waiting to infest any given crop and at multiple stages.

Brother Norbert informed me that soybeans hadn't done well in the Santarem area because of the ants that seem to favor bean sprouts as their favorite diet, especially when the bean sprout was just protruding through the soil. About twelve varieties of soybeans were available in Brazil, and all of these varieties had one thing in common. They all developed much denser foliage. Soybeans didn't store well because of the high humidity, and in storage, the beans tended to draw moisture. Brother Norbert advised that I try to use seed that had been developed for this area. He had learned this from experience, especially after trying seed from the United States for the first two years. Then he found that native-developed seed worked much better. A lot of progress had been in the development and growing of soybeans in Brazil, and I bet Brother Norbert played a huge role in its development

---

[7]   Bad chair

Brother Norbert's long-range plan was to supply all the local religious communities with his meat and produce and use all the grain to raise livestock. As for the natives, very few people had refrigeration that could handle the storage of a large beef or pork. On several occasions, it was very clear that the natives didn't intend to pay a higher price for the superior quality of corn-fed beef or pork.

While I was in Santarem, one of the natives brought in a sloth tied to a tree branch that he wanted to show off before he took it to market. A sloth had a walking speed of about one mile an hour, and the strength of its limbs was amazing. It was nearly impossible to pull the sloth down from a tree, and that was why they were seldom found on the ground. I estimated that the one I saw weighed about twenty-five pounds and appeared to be an adult. Their main diet consisted of fruits that grew high in the jungle. Mangos seemed to be one of their favorite. I felt sorry for the poor creature as it hung on the branch, and his face had the expression of a doomed person. By the look on his sad face, it was as if he knew his fate.

After spending nearly a month on the farm, I told Brother Norbert I was ready to continue upriver and start on some projects. I still had no idea what lie ahead, but I knew I could always count on Brother Norbert if I needed help. Brother Norbert said he hated to see me go because I made a pretty good ranch hand and I knew English, but he knew full well my mission. I am deeply indebted to this wonderful order and especially Brother Norbert.

CHAPTER 6

MANAUS, BRAZIL

Back into the air again on a DC-3 as I was bound for the city of Manaus, another five hundred miles upriver, I saw, in my opinion, one of the wonders of the natural world. I was fascinated to witness the marriage of the waters, where the Solomons, the main river body of the Amazon, converged with the huge river called Rio Negro, which has water stained like the shade of Coca-Cola. This marriage lasted for at least thirty minutes as we flew untold miles over these two giant rivers. Eventually, the Solomons swallowed up the jungle root-stained water as every drop turned into a muddy tan color. I learned the Amazon was made up from a network of seventeen tributaries, some over a thousand miles themselves, eventually all joining to flow into the ocean at Belem. The mouth of the Amazon is over two hundred miles wide as it enters the Atlantic. This river's huge volume affects the ocean's current over two hundred miles out into the sea. The Amazon, the second-longest river at 3,980 miles in length, is the largest river on Earth. This massive river was the home to twenty-five hundred species of fish, and nearly forty thousand plant species thrive along the banks. It's common to find the Amazon River over six miles wide at several points inland, and the river is much wider at times during the wet season. One-fifth of the freshwater that flows into all of Earth's oceans comes from the Amazon network. And I had an aerial view of it all flying into Manaus.

Manaus, located nine hundred miles inland from the Atlantic, was a thriving city from 1890 to 1920 due to the rubber boom. Latex, which was harvested from the jungle, was needed for making rubber tires to supply the fast-growing use of automobiles and trucks in the United

States and around the world. Jute, used for burlap bags and rope, was also gleaned from the jungle. Two factors brought this boom to a halt. An Englishman, Sir Henry Wickham, smuggled rubber tree seeds out of Brazil and started several plantations in Southeast Asia. Second, the development of synthetic rubber in 1920 brought the need for natural rubber to a near halt. Synthetics would also play a role in the reduced need for jute, a major export of Brazil. Everything has its zenith, and while money was plentiful in Brazil, the famous opera house was constructed, and Manaus was transformed into a beautiful city. The opera house, the Amazon Theater, was decorated on the inside with material and artists from Europe. The harp-shaped inside seating in the central hall could seat 640, and the auditorium had three floors and box seats. Toward the back, the stage curtain projected the painting of the "Marriage of the Waters" by Crispim do Amaral, which he completed in Paris before it was installed. On the outside, thirty-six thousand ceramic tiles painted in the colors of the nation's flag covered the dome.

While in Manaus, I stayed with two Papal Volunteers from Iowa, Tony and Dave. Both resided in a second-story flat right across the street from the park surrounding the famous structure.

In that very park, I witnessed a huge event called "folklorical" in which all sorts of people would dress in fantastic costumes to depict their origin. I saw huge headdresses made of brilliant feathers and flowers. Some were costumed as bullfighters; some were the bulls. I grabbed my camera and went into the park to take pictures. All participants were more than willing to pose, probably thinking I would make them famous. I marveled at the thought, *How could such a poor people spend so much on these costumes?*

I was scheduled to travel upriver on the Redemptorist boat, *The Alfonzo*, which was leaving in a few days. There I met another Papal Volunteer, John, also from the Diocese of Sioux City. John had come down from Coari to make supply purchases for the Papal Volunteers and Redemptorist Fathers in Coari. One of the supplies was cases of canned Spam. It was a real task to keep up with John as he scurried around Manaus to various outlets. I could tell John sure knew his way around. At one particular shop, John asked the shopkeeper for six light bulbs that were on the shelf. The shopkeeper said he would only sell us four.

Frustrated, John asked, "I see you have six, and I need six, so why not sell me the six?"

The shopkeeper relied, "Then I won't have any to sell."

It was a good thing that John had a very short haircut, or I believe he would have pulled his own hair out.

I studied John carefully for I knew I'd be living in the same house in Coari while we were there. John was an amazing person. By Brazilian standards, he was a giant of a man, six foot in stature and well over two hundred pounds. The Brazilian men would stop in the street and admire his large frame as he took up most of the sidewalk as he passed by. The men would always look down at his feet, which were usually clad in flip-flops. They were probably the largest feet these Brazilians had ever seen.

Being heavy and sometimes even fat in Brazil was a sign of wealth, and this was usually the desire of the women in Brazil, for it signified they were of wealth and well kept and was not in want of good food. I had a hard time understanding this concept after being in the United States all my life where most women strived to be slender. Another trait for those trying to impress everyone with their wealth was to allow the pinkie fingernail to grow to a ridiculous length. This was to prove to the world that they themselves wouldn't have to do manual labor, nor have they had to in the past. When these people would gesture toward something, they would always point with that elongated fingernail. Their vanity drove me crazy.

While in Manaus, I decided I needed a pair of dress slacks so I went to a store that sold them. I tried on several pairs, but they all seemed too tight of a fit. Between my broken Portuguese and the poor clerk, who couldn't speak English, I finally managed to buy a pair only after the clerk agreed to adjust the length of the legs. When I got back to the flat, I told Tony and Dave about my adventure. Tony realized I had my words for right and left mixed. It was no wonder the clerk couldn't figure out what was going on. I hurried back to the shop, but I was too late. The wrong leg had already been cut short. Needless to say, the shop owner was relieved when I paid for them anyway, and we both started all over.

Finally, it was time to set sail on the Redemptorist Fathers' boat bound for Coari 350 miles to the west. The town itself had about five thousand inhabitants, but if the surrounding area were included, twenty thousand people were in forty-five thousand square miles. The Redemptorist Fathers operated a grade school, high school, secondary normal school, and normal college in Coari proper.

Before the trip, John had gathered a month's worth of supplies for the fathers and the other Papal Volunteers in Coari. When we left the harbor, I couldn't help but notice the slum city floating around us. Thousands of people were living in small crafts of all descriptions, one tied to another, with makeshift shelters to protect the families from the sun and elements. The use of this area was unregulated and inhabited by the poorest of the poor, so it grew into huge proportions over the years. The potential for health problems grew with each new addition. The water below each craft provided the sewer as well as drinking water and water used for cooking and laundry. I was told that eventually the Brazilian government stepped in and eliminated the whole floating suburb some years later.

A very capable young boat pilot maneuvered around it all, and soon we were on our way upriver. Due to the fact we were going upriver, the pilot kept the boat close to the shore where there was less resistance to the fast-moving current of the Rio Negro. Before long, we left the city of Manaus behind us as we entered the main river, the Solomons, just before the night overtook us. Five of us were on board besides the boat captain, and we strung our hammocks out to get some rest as we chugged up the river. The temperature stayed mild all night, and that was a good thing. There was no way to seal the boat if the weather were cold. We slept, and the motion of the boat gently rocked us in our sleep.

Breakfast was consumed on the boat, and the boat pilot, not being politically correct, was called the "boat boy." He made a pot of stout coffee, which we dumped into our cups with several tablespoons of cane sugar. French-style baguette bread, which always came wrapped with a band of poor-quality paper, was sliced, and we applied our own choice of spread, whether a sweet jam or tomato-type paste laced with pimentos. To my surprise, it was good, and I tried every variety. Not only did the boat pilot have to steer the boat, it was his responsibility to prepare meals for the passengers, keep the boat clean, and get some rest, all without stopping the boat. Every now and then, the pilot would stop the boat and dive into the water to clean the weeds out of the propeller, increasing the efficiency of the engine and reducing vibration.

Being close to the shore, we were passing inhabitants all along the way, and the little kids would stand on the shore and wave to us as we went by. We commonly saw different kinds of animal skins tacked to the sides of their homes. These skins, products of the wild jungle, would then be sold to provide money for the family.

Most of the wildlife along the river's edge was comprised of birds, some with stork-like legs who were fishing along the banks. Many flocks of wild parakeets, parrots, and colorful macaws would take flight and noisily pass overhead. Occasionally, the boat pilot would point out alligators of all sizes as they slipped into the water for protection. We wouldn't have seen many of the wild creatures along the shore if it weren't for the pilot's trained, keen eyes. With his help, we got to see several different kinds of snakes that seemed to be at home in the water. The pilot spotted a very small variety of jungle deer. While traveling at night, he would train his spotlight on various places that usually produced eyes gleaming back at us, usually an alligator that was swimming close to the shore.

One common sight was long trains of small boats all tied to a larger vessel that would tow then upriver against the swift current. Almost all the small boats were the size of a large canoe and usually had a crudely thatched roof for protection against the sun. Sometimes, whole families would be onboard, and almost all of the small boats had no engines. When one of the small boats would reach its destination, they would simply pay the fee due and then release themselves, paddling to the shore. The fathers' boat never towed other boats, so it would easily overtake these floating trains as we proceeded to our own destination upriver.

To pass the time for the next few days, we read, napped in the sun on top of the boat's roof, or played cards. There seemed to be very little problem with mosquitoes, but we had to be very careful of a deerfly-like insect that would land on us and take out a pretty good chomp of exposed flesh, so it was unwise to doze for too long.

On this trip, I was invited to play cards and help consume some of the beer onboard. After playing cards for several hours, I slipped to the back of the boat where the bathroom was located by the roaring diesel engine. The door was latched on the outside to keep it from swinging with the boat's motion. I unlatched the hook from the eye of the lock and let the hook rest on the peg right above the lock. In I went and relieved myself in the makeshift commode, basically a wooden box with a toilet seat over a hole in the boat that allowed the dropping or urine to fall directly into the river. When I turned to exit the small toilet chamber, the door wouldn't budge. I pushed on the door at several locations, thinking the door was jammed. To no avail, the door wouldn't open, and I paused to take stock

of the situation. A very small window was in the room. Its only purpose was to provide ventilation. I squeezed my head through and shouted to the front of the boat, hoping someone would hear me. Twenty minutes of shouting produced nothing so I tried to pull my head back in. I discovered that shouting that long must have expanded my head because

I couldn't get it back in. I was feeling my ears starting to tear off my head when I pulled too hard.

How on earth could I get my head out of this small opening and yet can't get my head back in?

I envisioned workers having to cut the side of the boat open just to extract my head. When I mentally calculated the alternative, it renewed my fervor to get my head out of the window.

I was standing through this whole process, and I soon learned I couldn't sit down and rest, even if I wanted to, for I would choke. I knew I had to get my head back into the boat. After many attempts, I decided to try it again, even if it cost me my ears. I achieved success via turning my head ever so slightly and pulling hard without any regard to the pain and losses that might occur. Once my head was back in, I slumped, exhausted, back into the makeshift commode. Another hour went by, and I couldn't figure why someone wouldn't have missed me by now.

Surely they would want to at least finish the card game.

Suddenly, the bathroom door flew open, and my savior stood there, planning to pee. No one had any idea that I was missing or what I was going through. Apparently, everyone got tired of waiting for me to return to the card game. Full of beer, all had disbanded to take a nap. Thank God one of them finally had his bladder fill to overflowing, sending him scurrying to my rescue. This kind person then took the trouble to show me how to position the door latch so it couldn't vibrate down and relock the door.

Then he asked, "What happened to your ears?"

Since that time, I've been very careful to examine all bathroom door locks before entering. Call me paranoid.

River travel was not to be taken lightly, especially if one traveled on the commercial lines that operated up and down the Amazon. The main peril was the water supply, which was supposed to be boiled and filtered, but sometimes the staff would take a shortcut and just fill the drinking water tanks with water drawn directly from the river, so amoebas were always lurking. Ice was another source of impure water, and when ordering a drink, one had to specify "no ice." Every glass served was wet with droplets of water, and it made one ponder, "How many amoebas can be in one little drop of water?" With every plate used for eating, one always had to make sure it was dry before putting food on it.

I read Father Zenk's account of river travel in the month of February 1966 with amusement and empathy.

River travel along the Amazon is not the best. I was scheduled to leave Manaus, Brazil, bound for Coari, a trip of about three hundred miles, at noon on February 23 (which was also Ash Wednesday). Providentially for me, an American Redemptorist was also making the same journey and he was a veteran of five years along the Amazon. The boat did not leave at noon due to motor repair. Soon it was two p.m. and then it was four p.m. The usual answer to an inquiry about the time of departure was "another hour or two." At approximately six p.m. we were called for supper, and this was my first, and last, meal on that particular river boat. I wiped the fork with my handkerchief (we were given no napkin) and I noticed I had removed some foreign matter. Rice and beans and some type of meat were set before us. (We had been released from the obligation to abstain from meat that day, and it would have been difficult to observe it.) I ate only part of the meal, and after supper I walked over to see the kitchen. I noticed that things weren't as clean as they might be. About the same time, some water was needed on the boat. Was it for cooking, for washing dishes, or for coffee? I will never know. A bucket was dropped over the side of the boat (remember the boat was anchored, and it had been there for a few days), and after swishing the bucket back and forth a couple of times, up come the bucket of "nice, clean water." Having observed the source of the water, which in no doubt was used for various purposes on the boat; after viewing the kitchen, which must have been all of 5 feet by 5 feet; and after tasting the fare that was given for our opening meal on the boat, I decided I did not have the time or the strength to undergo a bout of dysentery in route to Coari. The boat was still in port at ten p.m., but shortly thereafter I fell asleep in my hammock. As a result, I do not know when the journey began, but it must have been near midnight when we headed upstream.

Father Zenk had just been appointed to replace Father Kevene as director of the Papal Volunteers in the Diocese of Sioux City. He was making the circuit in Brazil to see all the Iowa Papal Volunteers as well and to get the lay of the land.

We were on the river for two nights and three days before we entered the port of Coari. My first impression of the town from the vantage point of the water was, "What a combination of buildings!" They included large whitewashed buildings with red tile roofs, and then there was the opposite spectrum of homes, simple flat platforms raised two feet off the ground and a grass-thatched roof overhead. Most of these houses had only one wall thatched, and that wall usually faced the side the rain normally came from. Coari had a population of approximately five thousand people at that time.[8]

Coari had a radio station, a medical dispensary, a trade school, and a working hospital. There was also talk of soon having a paved road in the future as the prospect of an airport was not too far off. At the time, the only air travel had been an amphioxus plane that would land on the water, but it had ceased to exist.

Dysentery was a constant threat to everyone who lived in Brazil, especially those traveling from foreign lands. One time in particular, Padre Marcus's mother visited Coari. Somehow the conversation got around to asking the question if she'd had dysentery yet. She replied she was suffering from it that very moment and couldn't get too far from a bathroom.

I offered her some of my sage advice. "Don't race to the bathroom on every urge. Just force yourself to hold it as long as possible. That way, your body will have time to adjust, and after all, you are in charge of your body and not the dysentery."

The next day, I had the occasion to see her again. "How is my technique working?"

Her reply spoke volumes. "I'm sending you my laundry for that's what I think of your methods."

---

[8]   Coari has grown to over seventy thousand people in a span of a little of over forty years and now has a modern airport.

Author kneeling by the trunk he built for his journey to Brazil

My Bed with mosquito netting in the room assigned
to the author in Belem, Brazil

Author with his friend Raimundo who worked at Casa Central, Belem

A giant tarantulas that showed up one morning in the dining room of Casa
Central, Belem

Author sightseeing form a high rise in Belem, Brazil

A typical street found in Belem, Brazil

A bus used on the streets of Belem, Brazil

Brahma cattle that were treated for disease in Santarem, Brazil

Some of the Papal Volunteers on a spiritual retreat near Manaus, Brazil

Native ladies in costume for the local folk dance in Manaus, Brazil

A typical "river train" going up the Amazon River, right outside of Manaus, Brazil

A stray dog, watching a cow standing on the main street of Coari, chewing on a stalk of sugar cane.

One of John's pet macaws in the backyard in Coari, Brazil

Alphonso and Raul with several other men, constructing the first chicken house in Coari, Brazil

A lady purchasing a "married couple" of chickens from the
chicken project in Coari, Brazil

The first batch of chickens at three months

Author along with Padre Roi sowing rice by hand for the rice project

Francesca with the rabbit project

A local family doing their laundry during the dry season in Coari, Brazil

A young girl doing her laundry during the high water season

A small child's funeral in Coari, Brazil

A leopard skin drying the sun after being shot in the Amazon Jungle

Fr. Marcus (on the left) Ed, Margaret and John holding a large boa constrictor that was killed shortly after falling from the Church's ceiling

A crocodilo tinta or painted alligator, held captive, from the Amazon River the night before.

A peixes boyi fish that was highly sought after because its' flesh tasted similar to beef from feeding on the lush grass on the bottom of the Amazon

CHAPTER 7

HOME SWEET HOME

COARI, BRAZIL

As we continued into port, I couldn't help but wonder what I would be living in the next couple years. As we eased into shore, it seemed the whole town had come to see who was on the fathers' boat. There wasn't much entertainment in Coari, so meeting the boats was one thing to do. One of the large whitewashed buildings, which I spotted from the water, was to be my home. The house was a former nun's convent. Along with two other male Papal Volunteers, a married couple was also in the Papal Volunteers, John and Margaret. They occupied the downstairs where the kitchen, pantry, dining room, and their bedroom were located.

Upstairs was the where the men's bedroom was located. It was the largest room containing three single beds equipped with mosquito netting and three huge wardrobes. From my experience in Belem, I knew why all of the wardrobes were left wide open. Right off the bedroom was a large shower area with three shower stalls, all of which were finished in blue ceramic tile. Included in the bathroom were three toilets. On the other side of the bedroom area, a small room was equipped with a table for writing, reading, or studying.

Ray had already returned to Coari. He was a delightful roommate, as I predicted, and he always seemed to wear a brilliant smile. But he seemed to have his days and nights mixed up. He would stay up to at least three or four in the morning and sleep late into the day. His excuse for this behavior was because, back in Iowa, he had been on the night shift for a milk powder drying plant and his nocturnal habit stuck with him. Ray was able to pull it off. He hung a hammock in the study room, and with the aid of a kerosene mantle lantern on the table, with the door closed, he read most of the night. Also, when I was carrying on a conversation with him, he would invariably play like he didn't understand. I often felt he did this just to keep someone talking.

Ray's mission in Coari was teaching English in the city's high school, helping John the when needed, and traveling with the fathers when they went out on the river ministering to the various parishes along the river. Ray's helpfulness was invaluable to the fathers because he had a good grasp of the language and would help with the preparation for the many weddings, baptisms, and funeral masses that occurred with the fathers' visits.

My other roommate was Ed from Danbury, Iowa, an expert in construction, carpentry, and some mechanics. He was a jack of all trades. Ed was at least fifteen years older than Ray and I was. Ed helped keep us on the straight and narrow. The wisdom of Ed often showed, and it was great to sit around and talk to him. I considered him a confidant. Ed never forced his opinion on anyone, and one would have to ask Ed for his opinion in order to learn it. I spent many an hour talking about different projects that would be beneficial to the people of Coari, and I confided in him about how I missed everyone back home. Ed's brother, the priest in Iowa, got me into the Papal Volunteers. Sometimes, Ed and I would pool our resources in getting Ray straightened out. We would both be after Ray to pick up after himself because Ray would invariably leave a trail of dirty laundry when going to or from the shower. This went on for a long time, and Ray seemed deaf to our pleas.

One day, Ed said to Ray, "Every time I find any of your clothes lying around on the floor, I'm going to throw them away."

Ray never took Ed's threat seriously as Ray failed to change his ways. So Ed and I did exactly as Ed threatened, and every time we spotted some of Ray's laundry, we hid it away.

Several days, almost a week later, Ray stated, "I seem to be running out of underwear and socks, and I was wondering if you guys have had trouble with stuff getting lost in the laundry?"

Then Ed then said, "Ray, do you remember when I said I was going to throw your stuff away if I found them lying around?"

Ray got a really stupid look on his face as he murmured something to the effect that he did remember but didn't think anyone would ever do it. Ed waited until the next day before he turned over this large bag of dirty laundry. Ray was so relieved because there was no way he could find replacement clothes for his six-foot frame in Brazil. We never seemed to have that problem again. As for Ray's nocturnal habits, I don't believe anyone ever broke him of that.

John lived in the lower level of the house with his wife, Margaret. John's mission was to help the fathers with the Caritas program, the distribution of charitable goods that were sent to Brazil, mostly from the United States, through the Redemptorist Fathers. John also managed the purchasing responsibilities for the fathers and Papal Volunteers. His previous job in Sioux City was with the Pepsi Corporation as a route and purchasing manager, which prepared him for this position. John, being a large person, would often get loud when he tried to establish his authority or drive a hard bargain but seldom did his bravado work with the Papal Volunteers. We all knew John too well deep inside. All of us knew when to fold and when to hold when it came to dealing with this man. This even went for his wife, who would know how to get his temper up. Those two would get into some pretty good ones, and their spats often spilled out into the living area, despite all of us being present.

John kept two pet macaws in a nearby screened area. Despite all of his effort to get the birds to talk while he fed them, they would just turn their heads different ways as if listening intently but not repeating a single word for him. Invariably, when John would give up and come to eat breakfast with all of us, the birds would talk words to each other, and we could hear them. All of us, except John, would just crack up with laughter when the birds would imitate John and Margaret fighting. These birds had it down to every word.

Margaret's mission was to run the hospital that was connected to our building so her commute to work was only a few steps out the back door. This had its pluses and minuses. When it came to an emergency, Margaret would be right there in no time, but people would knock on the front door all hours of the day. Margaret worked under amazing difficulties at all times. A doctor was seldom on staff, nor did she have ample supplies of the right medications or access to trained help. Margaret had to train of her staff, and she found it difficult to convey the concept of germs and their existence all surfaces. Most Brazilians considered the hospitals as a last resort sort of thing, a place to die. Some of the fear came from the past on how some hospitals were run. Some of it came from the Brazilian people's profound belief in voodoo. From this, the hospital's reputation often perpetuated itself because, by the time somebody was brought in, it was often way too late. Margaret put her heart and soul into her work and would often have to make tough decisions quickly. If that person worsened or died, it bothered Margaret a lot, for she knew so much more could have been done if the patient had been admitted sooner. It was a common sight to see some of the locals waiting to see Margaret. While waiting, they would have white bath towels wrapped around their heads, filled with a white powder, to kill their head lice.

It was amazing how well all of us Papal Volunteers got along, and I don't recall a single time that we didn't respect each other. I'm not saying we didn't have our moments, but it never got out of hand. To pass our time, we played a special French card game called *coup forve*, and we never seemed to tire of it. It was especially nice that anyone could learn quickly and as many who felt like it could join in. Special occasions were never passed over as we all got into the celebration and had a good time. Some kind soul had left a record player and three records behind: two country albums by Fanon Young and George Jones and an instrumental by Henry Mancini. I literally wore out the Fanon Young record, and I knew every song by heart. I'm sure I drove everyone in the house mad when I would start to sing, and there was no stopping me for I still missed my home in the United States. It took me a long time to shake the hold that country music had on me after that.

Our housekeeper, a local Brazilian named Aparcedia, was a jewel. She handled the cooking, cleaning, and laundry with ease and always had a quick smile for all of us even though she had a heavy workload. It was especially fun to tease her and get her very dark brown eyes to flash while she pretended to be really mad. She worked together with John to keep the place running smoothly. She was a great lady.

Padre Ronald Weninger (Padre Marcus), a native of Allentown, Wisconsin, was pastor of our parish in Coari. A man of high energy, he was saddled with many duties in running the parish. Two other Redemptorist Fathers were assigned to Coari, and they were subject to Padre Marcus. One of the priests from the United States, Father James Fish (Padre Jamie), would help me in my duties working with the various youth groups. Two nights a week, I would open a small hall connected to the parish and play host/supervisor to various games for the local youth parishioners to join in. Padre Jamie would occasionally drop in and help refocus the youth as to why they were there and, obviously, get them off the streets at night as well. Padre Jamie would also organize soccer games to be played on the weekends, and I would often join in the play. I wore an elevated shoe on my left foot, and I always wore my boots because I couldn't run well without the aid of the built-up shoe. When I played soccer, the Brazilian boys always gave me plenty of room when they thought I was going to kick the ball with my left foot. There seemed to be little thought about one's race in Brazil, but I found a good deal of judgment was passed as to one's wealth and status.

When trying to figure out a project that would be the most beneficial to the people of Coari, Padres Jamie and Marcus had a lot of insight on what could be done. Ed was very knowledgeable and gave me much to go on. Ed always seemed to have the knack of using common sense when trying to figure something out. Ed was working on a project building a small chapel/meeting hall for the downriver town of Camera. He asked if I would like to accompany him to his project while I sorted out what I could do to contribute. I jumped at the chance to go.

Letter to Home
May 5, 1965

Hello to everyone at home from Coari, Brazil. I have been here in Coari about a week now, and the time has been filled with several meeting with the fathers who are stationed here in Coari. The purpose of the meetings was to look into possibilities for projects to do for the next two years or so. Tomorrow, another Papal Volunteer named Ed and I will go by boat to a small town called Camera to finish building a chapel that Ed started. This town is quite far into the interior, and we will be roughing it. I thought it couldn't get any rougher then what is here. I really wish I could be home for my brother Bob's wedding, but be sure to give him my blessings and congratulations. Be sure to kiss the bride a few extra times for me. It is events such as a wedding that make me question why I am here and instead not at home absorbing all the wonderful happenings. I'm sure I'll be able to make up for lost time when I get home. I'm taking lots of pictures, and I'll get them on their way as soon as possible. Love, Marvin

When we arrived in Camera, Ed showed me what was to be home for a few weeks. Ed assured me that we were in the best house in town. In fact, we were in the only wooden structure in town. No one could imagine my dismay when I saw the small shack that was to be ours. The structure had a tin roof, thin boards for sidewalls, and a wooden floor that had at least an inch of space between the boards. The structure itself was on stilts that held the building up about three feet off the ground. This meant every goat, pig, chicken, duck, goose, or pet dog would come to hide in its shade under the building. The spaces in the floorboards were supposed to be part of the ventilation solution, but as it turned out, the air coming up through the floorboards had a stench of the various animals trying to keep cool. During the day, the hot sun would heat the tin roof up many degrees so we couldn't sleep in the structure during the day. By nightfall, all our guests would leave from under the building to forage for food, and the roof cooled as well. The cool breeze came up through the floorboards, carrying the scent of animal waste.

The first and second surprises came when it was time to go to the bathroom. First, there was no bathroom per se. To facilitate the body's need for a bowel movement, one would arm himself with a roll of toilet paper and head into the jungle. One didn't have to walk far to be out of everyone's sight. The first time I went into the jungle to answer nature's call, I perched myself up on a small fallen tree. Boy that was a mistake. Fire ants quickly covered my backside and other parts, and it took some pretty good dancing and slapping to get them off me. I soon learned I would have to squat on my haunches to get the job done. If I spent too much time squatting, the second surprise came when vultures walked right up to me and started on their lunch before I could get out of there. When I gave the vultures some room, several would fight for the spoils as they took their sanitary duties very seriously.

After darkness set in, the sounds of the jungle increased, and it seemed as if all of the insects in the jungle were vying for sound space. It was as if seven different symphony orchestras were tuning up at the same time, and all would get increasingly louder so each individual instrument could be tuned and heard. To me, it sounded as if there were this kaleidoscope of sound all blending together to try to make some sort of music but only to tumble around the ears. The monkeys and birds were totally silent through this blur of sound, and in their silence, I imagined they were all listening intently to the symphony. The larger nocturnal animals that prowled the jungle floor at night were stealthily silent, such as the *onca*.[9] It was a common sight in these small interior villages to see animal hides tacked to their shanties to dry. I learned the jaguar was mostly killed when it would attempt to take some bait at a shotgun-rigged booby trap set in the jungle. Someone spotting the *pragesa*[10] high up into the trees would capture these slow creatures during the day. He would simply cut off the branch the sloth clung to. He would be very cognizant of the sloth's huge claws and sharp teeth. Birds, such as macaws and parrots, were captured at night. When caught, they were shoved in hollow pipes for transporting. Huge snakes would be captured day or night and especially so when the snake was in the water. While I was in Camera, one of the locals gave me some alligator teeth. I learned the teeth were given as a token of the esteem the local people had for us.

During that two-week stay in Camera, Ed's input helped me formulate what I was going to be doing the next two years. I would center my project on providing food for the Brazilian family. It was important to know what meat could be processed for eating and would have to be consumed in a day, as there was little or no access to refrigeration. I reminisced to Ed about the chicken farms in Belem that I had seen. I told Ed I was thinking about chickens as a project. Ed agreed to help me draw out the plans for my first chicken house, and he agreed to help build in trade for my work spent in helping him with his chapel in Camera. I returned to Coari with newfound purpose.

Letter to My Twin Brother, Darwin
May 6, 1965

Hello to my favorite twin brother. I survived a stay in a small town named Camera, and I'm now back in Coari. I'm happy to announce that I have some ideas from several discussions and the promise of help from some people. I decided one of my major projects will be raising chickens. A lot has to be decided yet, and the fathers here seem to very reluctant to commit to anything. Without their backing, I might as well fold up my tent and go

---

9 Jaguar
10 Sloth

> *elsewhere for they have control of everything. The locals have no idea what I have in mind so they, too, are tepid. Sometimes, one would get the impression that the people down here do not want to be helped, and I give you this example as related to me. Two men from Germany came to Brazil with their own money and purchased a tract of land. They planted numerous rubber trees for use seven years into the future. That is how long it takes for rubber trees to mature and start producing. Everything went along fine for the first seven years without a hitch, but on the seventh year, the Brazilian government came in and made it so difficult for these investors. The government acts like it wants to seize the whole operation just as the trees are ready to produce. I'm told that foreigners can never really own property or become a citizen with equal to the rights of a native-born citizen. I must close for now, and please write me how Duke is doing and if the "Tank" is still running. Oh, if that old car could talk, we would have to plug Dad's ears. Hi to all. Sending all of my love. Love, Marvin*

Sometimes, I could feel the suspicion in the local's eyes as they looked at me as if they were trying to figure out what I was really up to and what I was really doing here.

I sometimes asked myself, "What the hell am I doing here, and what am I thinking?"

At times, I did understand these deep-seated suspicions because the Brazilians were a very proud people. They felt a bit ashamed of people just coming to help, especially when they considered what we must have left behind. Almost all the Brazilian people really believed untold wealth was hidden deep in the jungle, whether it was diamonds, oil, or gold. I understood the gold part because of what I read about how Spain and Portugal had lined their churches and palaces with Brazilian gold.

I was feeling rather low and confused during that time, and then I received a letter from my dad.

Letter to My Dad
May 8, 1965

> *Hello, Dad. What a wonderful letter I just received from you. The letter did two things for me. First, it gave me the courage to press on, and your words counseling about me being the foreigner hit the mark. Secondly, your letter*

helped me to not despair, and lo and behold, while rereading your letter at the fathers' rectory here in Manaus, one of the priests approached me and said he was in contact with the Ford Foundation. They were very interested in my endeavors. So you see, Dad, your timely letter really helped, and I'm going to give it all I've got. Your loving son, Marvin

Farming itself was a real issue here in town or nearby here for the town sat on really heavy red clay. It was so dense that the soil was primarily used for making brick. Nothing had to be added to the soil to make these bricks for they would just cut the heavy red clay the size they needed, place the cut clay in a metal mold, haul it to a kiln, and fire it. Some of the most beautiful hardwood in the world fired the kiln. I was told that, a few miles out of town, the soil steadily improved for farming purposes.

Not all the news in Coari was bad, however, for we had a bit of excitement that we didn't expect to happen in this town. Pan Am Airlines had suspended flights to Coari some years before, so, much to our surprise, a plane descended out of the sky and landed on the water. Excitement rippled through the town, and everyone dropped what he was doing to rush down to the water's edge. I also got very excited, and I grabbed my camera and ran with the best of them. I got a few shots of this old Catalina airplane touching down and sending up a plume of water and spray. The plane looked old, but it was a welcome sight. Its presence created a circuslike atmosphere on shore.

All the little kids came running as well and gathered around us Papal Volunteers. They watched as we snapped photos of the airplane. Every time they heard the shutter click from the camera, they would all giggle and chatter among themselves and then crowd in a little closer and try to get their face into picture. Some of the more brazen children would go so far as to stick their faces in front of the camera lens without being asked.

Despite all of these encumbrances, I was still able to get off a few good shots of the landing and the small boats that rushed out to meet the plane. I was disappointed to learn that this flight had no mailbags but the next flight tomorrow would.

―――――――――

With the thought of producing small things, I started a rabbit-raising project, thinking a rabbit could be slaughtered and devoured the same day without refrigeration. In keeping with the Papal Volunteers model, two young people were chosen to be in charge of the rabbit project, keeping in mind that when, these young girls were ready, they would take over the entire project. If this project were to succeed, this would be one of the few businesses that women would run.

As the Papal Volunteers worked on their projects, we would all try to help each other when we had the opportunity. I once had the opportunity to help Margaret. I was passing through the hospital, and Margaret was trying to remove a piece of pencil lead that had gotten so far into this child's arm muscle that it was lodged very deep into the boy's arm.

I casually advised Margaret, "There must be a better way of performing this than what you're using."

The next thing I knew, here I was attempting to dig it out as Margaret went back to work with another patient. Needless to say, it was harder than it looked, but after some effort, the patient walked out cured.

Letter to My Mom
June 2, 1965

Hello, Dear Mother. I hope all is well there as is here. One complaint I do have is the mail is taking at least a month to get to me, and I do hope it is not taking that long to get to you. In your last letter, you asked about the meals. We seem to get by, but when I get home, here is how I want the table set. First, have two gallons of cold milk ready, four loaves of your homemade bread still warm and fresh out of the oven, and at least a half-pound of real butter. A thick, juicy corn-fed beef steak or a pork roast would do. A large dish of salad for I learned to like salad down here, and please have a large slice of pumpkin pie as only you can make, Mom. Make sure the pie is topped with a mountain of real cream whipped and, in it, just a touch of vanilla flavoring, like you used to prepare. My little sister can make the whipped cream, but you, Mom, must do the rest. I have to stop before I drown in my own saliva, and by the way, that was just lunch. And now for dinner. The pictures I have enclosed include a picture of a small girl, one of the little girls who kept following me around for she thought I was a priest and I should bless her. The only way I could get her to go back to her house was to take a picture of her. It isn't unusual to see a small band of kids following the fathers around when they emerge from the rectory, and all the little people will clamor for a blessing. The next shot is of my canoe that I purchased for the purpose of traversing over the water to the chicken project when the water is up. Enjoy. Love, Marvin

Right after mailing that letter, all of the Papal Volunteers left for Manaus where we met up with the other Papal Volunteers of the area. It was a good break for me, and I got to meet a lot of other Papal Volunteers and discuss our trials and rewards on all of our respective projects.

When I got back from retreat in Manaus, I was surprised to be presented with three grey rabbits that had been sent up from Belem. I had no idea they were coming, and I had no idea who the benevolent party was. The poor things had been in a box no bigger than a beer case for two whole weeks while the fathers, who cared for them while we were gone, were afraid to handle them. As you can imagine, I was also so unprepared because I had no rabbit food or even a place for them to live.

John, Lucia and Francesca, the two girls picked for the project, and I built two rabbit hutches to house the rabbits on their arrival. We started with two old bunk bed frames, and each hutch was made with an enclosure on the rear side as a refuge from the elements. Each hutch was designed for nesting. The hutch had to be designed in such a way that the female could feel entirely safe from predators while spending time giving birth and nursing her young. The hutches were to have adequate ventilation so the young wouldn't die from the heat while confined to the nesting quarters. The front of the cage was designed to be strong enough to resist predators, provide good ventilation, and have a floor capable of allowing the rabbit droppings to fall through to the ground, making it easier to clean. One of the hutches had been portioned in half so a male and female could be beside each other, allowing them to become acquainted with each other without actually being together. So when it came time for mating, the pair would be less likely to fight.

As soon as the first hutch was finished, we put the pair of rabbits in it right away, and then we had to go down town and search for food. How these rabbits arrived, surviving the long trip from Belem, made me appreciate the phrase, "God works in mysterious ways!"

With two rabbit hutches, two male bucks, and a female doe, our project began. John was invaluable with his help in training the young ladies in the care of the rabbits and planning for the future care in the event little bunnies were on their way. Due to the extreme heat, we knew it would difficult to get the rabbits to breed.

On June 23, a really popular local young man died of hepatitis rather suddenly, and I was asked to go to his home and take photos. Usually, photos weren't the normal process at the time of death. because the lack of equipment and the life of stored film in the tropics. This young man, a good friend of the fathers, was a sort of deejay at the fathers' radio station. He was well liked and known throughout the area.

When I entered the home about three hours after this man's death, the already present smell of death bowled me over. The body of this young man was in a prone position. His hands were tied with cord to hold them in a prayerful hand fold. Large, heavy Brazilian coins were placed on the eyelids to hold them shut until rigor mortis set in. The room where he lay was very dark, and all sunlight was blocked out, but lighted candles surrounded the body. The Brazilians could sometimes be very superstitious, and I was told the candlelight would keep out the evil spirits. As no outside light could come in, no evil could be carried with the light rays. The body was carried to the cemetery almost immediately after I finished taking photos and, I must say, not a moment too soon due to the lack of the embalming process and the oppressing heat. A funeral Mass was celebrated the next morning with an empty wooden casket that was draped with a black cloth representing the corpse.

The death rate of children was very high in Coari, and it was said that 60 percent of children didn't reach the age of five. Most of this was due to substandard nutrition, and in the child's weakened state, almost any childhood disease would be fatal. When a funeral did occur for a small child, the father would carry the corpse in his arms to the cemetery. Hordes of small children would noisily join in the march carrying the lid of the coffin while an adult would carry the small, roughly hewn pine box. Upon arriving at the cemetery and after a certain amount of ceremony, the child was placed in the box, the lid was placed on the coffin, and two men on each end holding ropes would lower it into the grave. Once all the prayers were said, the small children would start kicking the dirt into the hole, squealing and celebrating as they did so. It occurred to me that a funeral was a celebration, not a sad thing. This made me examine my own faith in regard to earning heaven. To mark the grave of a small infant, a wooden headstone in the shape of a baby's crib was left to mark the spot where the infant lay.

One story I was told (which I do not claim to be true but possible) was about when one of the good sisters of the nearby convent had been ill and near death for some time. When she died, she was prepared for immediate burial in the usual way. The funeral procession quickly formed, and the long trek to the cemetery snaked its way out of town. Thousands of people had reportedly joined the procession to pay their respects. The journey was long and slow as four pallbearers who struggled with their load carried the coffin as someone else carried the lid. According to the story, everyone was halfway up the hill to the cemetery when the good sister suddenly sat straight up and looked around. Screams and panic gripped the crowd, and in a split second, thousands of people scattered down the hill, running as fast as their legs could carry them. Even the pallbearers dropped the coffin and ran. The person carrying the lid followed suit. Total silence set in as only the priest was left with the remains, the coffin, and lid. It must have taken a lot of tall talking to convince someone to come and help the father get the poor sister back to the convent, as she indeed was not dead. Apparently, the sister had come back to life, aided by all the jostling on the way to the cemetery. By the time they got the sister back to the convent, she lapsed into a coma and officially died that night. The nuns were very careful not to call another hasty funeral, and the crowd for the second funeral was much smaller for the second time to the cemetery.

I did see full-blown panic when a Sunday Mass was filled to capacity. Right during the very silent part of the service, a scraping sound was heard from the termite-infested panels in the ceiling of the main church. They had been installed to protect the people below from falling dirt and debris. Suddenly, a panel burst open, and down came this twenty-foot boa constrictor, crashing and twisting on the floor. Panic set in, and in a short second, one could only hear the patter of feet and screams fading away. Only the father stood at the altar unmoved and continued praying the Mass as the snake headed for shelter out the door. Several hours later, the boa constrictor was killed when someone spotted it by the generator building. It was learned that the snake was probably deliberately placed in the ceiling some years before to help control rats and bats that frequented the belfry. To authenticate the event, Padre Marcus, Ed, John, and Margaret did a photo op with the dead snake. Snakes weren't well thought of and would be quickly dispatched when sighted in any location, as this one learned the hard way.

I also formulated another plan to plant a vegetable garden. A seed source and seed for a nutritious menu had to be located. All this came about with the aid of Padre Jamie, who had some knowledge on what was available and where. The order was placed through a person who was going downriver to Manaus for other business. It always amazed me that, when one would learn of someone going to a larger city or even perhaps the States, it wasn't considered a problem or inconvenience to expect someone to find something, perhaps buy it, bring it back in personal luggage, and expect nothing for it. The person ordering the seed had to seek several places, gather the different needs, and carry it back to Coari.

While waiting for the seed to return, I took a shovel and turned up a fairly large garden. The spot I picked had a sunny location, and it was located where a tropical grass was growing as a part of the lawn, so it wasn't too difficult to till. I went up into the church steeple, the bedroom for hundreds of vampire bats, and gathered bat guano. I spread a thin layer on the soil before turning, and it worked nicely. The garden plot itself was approximately two hundred square feet. The ground sloped ever so gently, so I didn't expect much erosion when the heavy tropical rains would soon come.

Several days later, the seed arrived, and I planted long rows of varieties of peas, string bean, tomatoes, lettuce, beets, Swiss chard, turnips, and some Brazilian varieties. Confident that everything would soon be up because there was ample daily rain and the warm tropical sun would warm the soil to a nice growing temperature, I checked the plot several times a day. If worrying and fretting could get seeds to grow, my garden would be outstanding. And sure enough, after four or five days, I could make out rows of small bumps in the soil where seed was trying to push their tender leaves into the warm Brazilian sun. By the next day, almost all the seeds had sprouted, and distinct green rows had taken shape. I knew a nice, warm rain would come daily around four o'clock to keep everything growing along just fine. On the third day, after the first leaf emergence, there was a beautiful stand of everything all in pristine rows. I felt I was experiencing the same feeling that God must have felt on the sixth day of Creation and looking over his work.

That night at evening meal, I bragged about how easy it was, and I couldn't understand why this hadn't been done sooner. I invited everyone at the table to join me in the morning, right after breakfast, to come to the garden with me and view a vista like nothing like it before. That night, I dreamt of sweet corn on the cob, tomatoes the size of dinner plates, carrots round and at least a foot long, radishes so succulent that one wouldn't need anything else, and fresh peas by the tub full, waiting to be processed and eaten. The fresh greens, oh my!

I hurried everyone through breakfast because I knew that, once the other Papal Volunteers went through the door to their work, I wouldn't see them all day. Even nocturnal Ray got up after some urging. Like a band of curious tourists, we all converged on the hallowed area, and to my horror and shock, not a sprig or dot of green was to be seen. Everything was gone, completely gone. Not even a sign of any rows, sprouts, or anything except the red clay soil I had tilled and planted so carefully.

"What could have happened?" I queried everyone as I studied faces for a clue of perhaps a trick or some kind of wisdom that could be shared with me.

Nothing. No could offer me anything as I studied the ground, looking for the marauders' tracks. Again, nothing. The ground looked unmolested and at peace with nature.

I knelt in the cool soil and used my hands to ask, "What happened?"

As I sunk them into the garden dirt, the soil revealed nothing to me. I found some sprouted seeds with the roots still attached. When I turned around, everyone had gone without a word, leaving me in my despair and shock. I was on my own, for no one had anything to offer. I knew I must get to the bottom of this if the project were to survive.

After checking with Padres Jamie and Marcus, who also had nothing to offer, I was on my own. After returning to the garden plot several times during the day, I could see some sprouts trying to replace their loss by late afternoon. By evening, I could definitely see some rows again and some latecomer seeds were starting to show themselves.

Maybe, just maybe, we'll have a garden yet.

I was glad I hadn't appointed a partner/foreman to the project to share in the mystery and disappointment.

The next morning, quite early before Mass and breakfast, I slipped out to the garden all by myself, hoping to see the plants in their continued comeback. As I peered through the early dawn light, I could see nothing. Absolutely nothing. There were no signs of any green foliage once again. It was as if something had snipped the new growth away with a very fine cutter of some kind and then carried off the snipping. I was once again bewildered and just sick with disappointment.

That morning after breakfast, I went back to Padre Jamie, and he recommended I see Manuel, the person who helped keep the grounds around the fathers' house and the nuns' convent. When I located him, I tried to relay my problem in my poor Portuguese. After many gestures and hemming and hawing, I finally convinced him to see for himself.

As we both gazed over the garden plot, Manuel muttered, "*Formiga!*"[11]

Then Manuel pointed out these very fine intricate little trails that wound through the grass below. Manuel spoke fluent Portuguese, but he spoke too fast and excitedly for me to keep up. Finally, he was reduced to motions and gestures as he kept repeating "*Formiga!*" As it turned out, Manuel was trying to tell me that very large ants had been invading the garden at night. These ants were so large and powerful that they would cut off the foliage right at the base of the plant and carry it to their nest. Worker ants first cut and cleared two very fine paths through the lawn grass, starting from their nest, which was at least one hundred feet away, all the way to the garden plot. These worker ants cleared this path so the other ants, carrying the "good stuff," would be able to travel swiftly and with wide loads. When Manuel and I followed the trail from the garden to the nest for one hundred feet or so, we found a smooth, surfaced hole in the ground that measured two inches across. A bare patch surrounded the hole and several mega ants, that looked like they had taken steroids, paced around the hole.

Manuel was able to say in Portuguese, "*Grande problema!*"[12]

These ants were huge, red, large, and bulky and must have measured at least an inch long. They were ready to fight to the last ant to defend their lair. Manuel took a small stick and poked at the ants acting as sentinels, and

---

[11] For-me-ga
[12] Big problem

these ants reacted with rage as they attacked the stick. They immediately started to scamper up the stick with their pinchers wide open and ready to sink into the flesh of someone or something. At the same time, the ants must have sounded some kind of alarm that was inaudible to us humans, or perhaps they sent out message through scent, but whatever they used, the reaction was immense. Within seconds, Manuel and I were retreating, I in my heavy leather boots and Manuel in his dilapidated flip-flops. The circle of angry ants grew increasingly larger as the nest emptied of these fierce insects that were just spoiling for a fight. These ants were so fierce that they would stop at nothing. Several times, I had seen young boys form a circle and pit two of these giant ants against another ant the same size. Usually, it was a fight to the death, which often didn't take too long, and the boys would try to pick the winner when the ants were placed into combat.

Manuel and I gave the ants their required distance as we headed to Padre Jamie for interpretation of Manuel's excited chatter. When we reached Padre, he explained Manuel was saying these ants ruled the jungle and surrounding areas. They would destroy anything they liked by cutting sizeable pieces of foliage off the plant and hauling it off to their nest. Manuel went on to describe how, at night, one could find a cleared trail of solid red mass of ants moving to the food source and then this green trail of foliage being carried back to the nest and pulled down into the ground to be stored in the nesting area.

After much detailing and persuasion, it was decided to forget the garden project for the time being or at least until I could develop a foolproof plan to hold off the ants and other insects. It didn't make sense to me to start using pesticides and herbicides on a family garden plot, for I felt the long-range effect would probably do more harm than good.

I later learned some interesting fact on those huge ants. The name of these huge insects is ants with trap-like jaws, whose main function is cutting leaves. At first glance, one would believe that these huge ants were cutting and hauling these leaves to feed an endless appetite of huge ants with a large need for nourishment. The real reason for the parade of half-moon leaf parts is not for supplies at all but to create a kind of compost, on which a moss like fungus is grown for food. Once inside the nest, worker ants that were smaller in size would chew up the leaves into small little balls. Once this was done, the ants planted small amounts of fungus on the chewed-up leaves and waited until a white, fuzzy fungus appeared. That was harvested and fed to their larvae. The fungus was also the sole source of food for the whole colony. In Paraguay, a photo was taken from an airplane that revealed an intricate network of "highways," some paths as wide as six to eight inches that radiated out in all direction from the main mound of dirt surrounding the nest. Some of the nests would go as deep as twenty feet. Once inside the nest, any insect, no matter the size, was usually dead meat upon approach, for these ants had very large and incredibly strong pinchers to defend them in time of battle. The more I learned about these ants, the more I knew I had made the right decision to just plain give up.

———

With the failure of that project still stinging, my thoughts turned to chickens, another project that was smoldering in the recesses of my mind. I hatched this idea while I spent the couple weeks downriver with Ed, and to his credit, he helped me formulate the concept. I remembered the Japanese farmers in Belem and how they constructed their chicken coops above ground. I remembered some of the building materials they used, and I knew these very same techniques would work fifteen hundred miles upriver.

I had already approached the fathers for a small plot of land that I could use to build a chicken house large enough to house one hundred chickens, and the fathers came through. Right across a small inlet of water were Brazil Nut trees, or the Brazilian name, castonia trees, that grew to one hundred feet in height. When I was still in the States, this was the land I was told I would get to farm, but as it turned out, the trees produced a cash crop that we know as Brazil nuts, and it was against the law to cut them down. So when the jungle was cleared, the trees were left standing on the approximate five to seven acres.

It was such a great relief to have John overseeing the rabbit project and the two very dedicated women helping him for I would be focusing my attention on the chicken project. I wanted to raise something small that could be slaughtered and consumed the same day, and the idea of chickens fit the bill. A small amount of cattle was raised in Coari, but when one was slaughtered, the whole town was notified so all the meat could be sold early in the morning on the same day. These same cattle were allowed to roam freely in the city streets and parks, and it was common to see the same stains on their necks where vampire bats had clung to their necks the night before.

Apparently, the fathers' connection with the Ford Foundation paid off, and I was in the chicken business. Ed, who I helped in Camera, had gotten involved in drawing up plans and speculations on my first chicken house. It was agreed that I could build on the fathers' land. The good news was that Ed got so excited with his drawings and all about the prospects of the building that he volunteered to help get me started. I was sure that, if I played my cards just right, I would get most of it done under Ed's guidance. Maybe there would be some kind of a Huck Finn thing.

Before the chickens could arrive, I had a lot to do. First, I had to recruit some project partners and get them involved and excited about the idea of going into business. The knowledge of Coari that the Redemptorist Fathers had gleaned over the years became invaluable to me. After all, the parish had been there for many years, and the fathers worked closely with their flock of people. They would know who would be just right for this endeavor. Two young men, Raul and Alphonso, were chosen. When I first met them, I could sense the doubt, or perhaps they were just straining to understand my Portuguese when I spoke to them about the future and role they would play in the chicken project. I had to leave them under the direction of Ed as I was to leave for Manaus to retrieve our first batch of chickens that had been ordered.

In July, the rainy season was just about over, and the Solomons had just about reached its crest. According to the locals and other Papal Volunteers, the river was very high that season, but it wasn't at a record. The bay nearly surrounding most of Coari was very full and at least a mile wide at the mouth of the river. The water would now start to recede until the bay eventually would go completely dry. During this dry season, a beautiful lush grass, know as butter grass, would emerge, and all the cattle in the surrounding area would gather to graze on the grass until the river would start to rise again the next season. If I had some money and backing, I would go into the cattle business and erect a silo of some sort, fill it with this lush grass, and feed it to the cattle during the season when that lush grass was gone and covered by water.

I was supposed to get the first batch of chickens from Manaus while I was at retreat, but the fathers didn't come through with the funding so I returned to Coari "empty-nested," so to speak. Not too long after that, it sounded like the deal was back on track. I found myself preparing to return to Manaus. The plan entailed me going back to Manaus to procure the little chicks and care for them on their trip back upriver, to making sure they were fed and watered.

Letter to My Twin Brother, Darwin
July 2, 1965

Hello to my favorite twin brother. The mail seems to take forever lately, and by the time you get this, I will be on my way to Manaus to pick up our first batch of hybrid chickens and gather some needed supplies for everybody in Coari. The chickens should arrive in a few days, and then I will turn right around and care for them on the trip back. I ordered the chickens from

Sao Paulo, three thousand miles away, a whole week ago, and they were to be flown to Manaus last Saturday, but the chickens failed to arrive. I'm told they will be here in a couple days if all goes well. The difficult part will be getting them from here to Coari for they will be transported by the fathers' boat upriver. I will be the one taking care of them. In the meantime, I'll have to seek out feed for the next month or so. Not only is it difficult to find feed that isn't already moldy because most of the feed is transported in the hold of small ships where water can settle in these boats, but it is also difficult to keep the feed from molding due to the high humidity down here. I will keep you posted. How is your love life progressing? I bet the truth is that you have to beat the girls off with a stick, especially after you got your new Chevy. Ha, ha. Be sure to not spend one minute worrying about my welfare for everyone is so good to me. I know I'm in good hands. Your loving twin brother, Marvin

---

On July 5, everything went as planned, and the box of one hundred chickens was turned over to me at the airport in Manaus. With the aid of a ride from the fathers in Manaus, I was driven from the airport straight to the fathers' boat that was tied to its mooring. We were to set sail as soon as I stepped on board with the box of a hundred baby chickens. Being the fact this was Brazil, the trip was delayed until the next day. Several bags of chicken mash had already been delivered to the boat, and I first gathered some feed for the small chicks. I set about the task of finding shelter at one of the Papal Volunteers here in Manaus.

Letter to Home
July 7, 1965

Hello to everyone at home. How is everything going? All is well here, and I've been having a good time traveling and waiting for our first batch of chickens. The chickens arrived today. Boy, are they big and strong for just being six days old. Their hatch was listed as July 1, and that's a good day for it was Mom's birthday as well. These little guys were flown by commercial jet from Sao Paulo, and when I got them, I first took them out of their shipping box where I was staying and fed them. At first, I got a few complaints about having these chickens out of their box and pooping everywhere, but I put newspaper down and cleaned up after them. Now everyone comes to see them, and they seem to enjoy them as much as I do. I feared the next three days going upriver by boat and trying to feed them and keep them warm for it gets really cool at night. The wind blows right through the boat. I ordered one hundred chickens, and that is exactly what I got at a cost of thirty cents apiece, which included the freight to Manaus. I feel the cost is fair, but the feed around here is very expensive. Tell everyone hello and remember me in your prayers as I play "Mother Hen" the next few days. All of my love, Marvin

---

As planned, we shoved off, bound for Coari in the late afternoon of July7. In the back engine room, I set up some small boards to serve as barriers so the little peeping chicks wouldn't stray. I scattered some feed on the newspaper and gently lifted out the contents of each quarter of the box. A lot of peeping went on at first as chicks huddled together; fearing the engine noise, but then one bold chick discovered the food at his feet and started to peck away at the scattered feed. Soon all the chicks were involved with pecking and scratching in the feed. For water, I borrowed a few bowls we used for meals, only after promising I would completely wash them before returning them to the storage rack. All the chickens ate hardily and drank their share of the filtered water. Scooping them up, twenty-five to each square, I placed them back in the box and let them spend the night where it was warmer in the engine room. This ritual continued three times a day throughout the trip, which lasted for three days and two nights. I soon realized that not everyone was happy to share their space with little chickens. Not everyone thought of them as cute. As

I cared for them, I harked back to the days when my mother would take care of the little chicks in the brooder house in Iowa, many, many years ago. As I reminisced, I was sure I would be able to draw on those past experiences from her.

The boat sounded its horn as we entered the lagoon waters off Coari. The banks at the port started to fill with thousands of people, all wanting to see the chickens. I think they expected to see full-grown hens and roosters cluttering the main deck, all ready to walk the plank to shore. It seemed like the whole population of Coari was there, craning their necks to see. After the boat docked and was tied up, I walked up the plank[13] carrying the box of one hundred little chicks.

All the murmuring among the crowd fell into a hush as someone asked, "Where are the chickens?"

I knelt on the bank and opened the box for all to see. Whispered tones from the crowd turned into some angry statements. Even I, with my poor grasp of Portuguese, could tell that the crowd was unhappy at the site of one hundred chickens huddled in one small box. They were perceived to be one hundred orphans. Raul and Alphonso, the two boys on the project, had shown up and stood in front of the crowd. I could see their prideful faces turn into surprise and then into quizzical expression and then fear. I knew something had gone wrong, and for the moment, I couldn't figure out why. I hurried on my own and walked up to the house with my box of little chickens. I couldn't help but notice that Raul or Alphonso didn't accompany me, but I was confident they would be there first thing in the morning to get involved.

On the trip back to Coari, my one hundred passengers made it well. Not one died, even though the trip was really hard on them. These chickens were of every different color, and many of them were a combination of colors. The official title of these chickens' pedigree was "High Cross," and I felt that pretty well described their mix.

Margaret met me at the door and demanded to know what I was thinking, bringing the chickens into the house. Then she wanted to know how long those chickens would be in the house, and I assured her that it was just overnight.

---

[13] The boat deck was lower than the riverbank.

The next morning, the feeding ritual was repeated, but we were on terra firma this time and, better yet, without the engine noise. It was amazing how fast the little downy chicks were growing in just a matter of a few days. Their food intake had already doubled, and, of course, the amount of chicken poop had doubled as well. I could see signs of feathers emerging, especially around the wings and tail. It was getting on to ten in the morning, and still no project boys had appeared.

A cold front had moved in, and the nighttime temperatures were getting down to at least sixty-five degrees. It might not sound that cold, but it was for the Brazilians living in their houses often with only one or two walls. The locals had no warm clothes, and if things didn't change for the warmer, many people would become ill. I knew I couldn't take the chickens to the chicken house on the other side of the lagoon, even though they weren't welcome in our home either.

The next morning, I talked to Padre Marcus about the people's reaction, and he revealed that the whole town was astonished I had played a part in making one hundred chickens orphans. The Brazilian people, for the most part, are very family oriented, and I had effectuated the unspeakable act of tearing these little chicks away from their loving mothers. Padre Marcus suggested I go see the boys' mothers and persuade them, through their mothers, to return to the project. Padre Marcus wisely pointed out that it appeared the problem was with the boys not understanding about the project. This had to be corrected, or the project would be doomed. Padre Marcus also added that the solution could only be achieved through the boys, so off I went to convince the boys to come back.

Raul's mother was a wonderful person and trusted my motives, and she rationalized that these chickens had been on their own for a long time now and perhaps they were over their trauma. She would convince her son to return. I couldn't find the other boy's home despite a lot of searching.

I returned to our house to feed the chickens once again, and then Margaret put her foot down, reminding me that time was up and the whole house was starting to smell like a chicken coop. She said something had to be done as I begged for one more day, and being a kind soul, she gave in. I didn't have the heart to tell Margaret that the first chicken house was far from completion, and I knew I had to take it a day at a time.

The next morning, lo and behold, Raul and Alphonso finally showed up and asked what they could do. I showed the boys how to take the chicks out of the box and how to water them. Then we departed to the work site where the first building was in the process of being built. As we made our way over to the chicken site, many people came to their front doors to watch us pass. These same people, who I had passed on numerous occasions, seemed a lot less friendly then before.

Upon arriving at the project site, the boys were very proud of the work they had done while I was downriver because the chicken house was almost ready. We sat on the floor, and I explained to them that, when eggs hatch, the little chicks soon lose their attachment to their mothers. From the troubled looks on their faces, I could see the boys weren't buying it. Even if they understood, they knew it wouldn't be easy to convince others. Then a thought occurred to me.

I said, "Look at it this way. These one hundred chickens are like students in a boarding school, and we are here to provide for them and teach them how to live in the interior of Brazil. When they grow up, they will stay here and have families of their own."

This scenario seemed to work well with both boys as both were very familiar with boarding schools, and they seemed so relieved. It was if a very heavy burden had been lifted from them. It wasn't long before the boys were back to being themselves and chattering and bantering back and forth like normal teenagers. I also convinced them that they had to be the ones to tell everyone what they knew about the student theory and the little chicks were eager to be here and their parents were very proud to send their offspring to "chicken school" so far away.

Within days, I could tell the boys were doing their assigned task of spreading the word because casual observers seemed a whole lot friendlier once again. In that same talk, I explained this project was so different from what had been done before and they themselves must develop a passionate loyalty to the project.

The chicken house was nowhere near being complete, and worse yet, construction was going very slowly, so we kept the chickens in the front entrance room of the Papal Volunteers' home. I could feel that Margaret was unhappy. Every day before going to the construction site, the boys would show up at the house and help care for the chicks by gently taking them out of the box, scattering feed on their newspapers, and setting out fresh water. Then they would carefully put them back into the box before heading off. I felt we would only be doing this for a few days, and soon the chicken house would be complete. Besides, the cold spell hadn't eased, and the chickens were safer in the house.

Letter to Home
July 21, 1965

Hello to everyone at home. All is well here as I do hope they are there. I feel bad that my letters are taking so long, but I guess we will just deal with it. The chickens in our house are getting a lot of complaints, and I'm feverishly trying to get our first chicken house built. I have four Brazilian workers who are under my direction, and my job is to keep them busy and for me to look busy myself. Ed, who I helped in Camera, is overseeing the whole project, and I really cherish his help. So far, we have gathered the lumber we need from the jungle, and we have it all carried out of the jungle to the site. The ground posts have all been dug and set for the foundation. Tomorrow, we are to complete the framework and put up the thatch over the roof. The thatch will go up quicker for we are using a very long branch of fernlike leaves. Each branch is about seven feet long, and all we have to do in the process is lay several layers over each other and tie them to the rafters as we go. The sideboards will be split bamboo, and we will nail each bamboo halfway to the frame. The nailing process is the hardest part because bamboo is really hard to nail, especially so when split in half. I know the solution is to be able to predrill the bamboo, and I sure could use some electricity over here, but that is out of the question. I will keep you posted as we progress. Love, Marvin

To find building supplies, we would go into the jungle almost every day to gather wood, and it was no small feat. All of our building supplies came from the jungle because we couldn't afford to purchase them locally. The nearby locals had gleaned most of the desirable materials we needed for their own projects over the years. We had to go more than three miles into the jungle to find what we wanted, and then we had to carry out what we cut. My big, heavy leather boots gave me comfort when traversing the jungle like we did. Many different types of dangers filled the jungle, but it was thrilling as well. When one was in the heart of the jungle, it was much cooler because of the jungle's canopy, formed by trees that pushed up two hundred feet or more to form a crown on top and absorb the sunlight. Below the canopy was a tangle of large vines that clung to the tree's bark and cascaded down in disarray. Ferns and low-light plants of all kinds, which grew everywhere and made passage very difficult, created a mat on the jungle floor.

While walking a jungle path once, Raul commanded, "Mario,(my Brazilian name) *para!*"

It meant I was to stop, which I did. With a swift slash of his machete, Rual sliced off the snake's head that was inches from my face. The snake was identified as the deadly bushmaster, which was known for killing anyone who was bitten. I started to tremble and sweat all the more when it came to me how close I had come. One also had to be very careful and not to step over objects, such as fallen trees, for snakes and huge spiders often used these very places for shelter. These creatures didn't take it kindly to being disturbed. Leaves and debris on the floor of the jungle often covered many of the deep holes that had been burrowed out by land locked creatures. If one would slip into one these holes, while walking, it could have serious consequences, such as a sprain or torn ligament. If the jungle floor started to give away, while walking, you would have to try and jump or hop forward.

The boys really enjoyed showing me things in the jungle and explaining their uses. Boys being boys would sometimes get carried away with their stories in trying to scare me, and when they did, they didn't know when to stop until I revealed I was on to them. For one lesson, one of the boys scampered up a banana tree and cut down a small bunch of ripe bananas with his machete. We took a break, and I started peeling a banana to enjoy. Out of the corner of my eye, I noticed both boys were snickering to each other as I peeled my first banana. I couldn't figure out what was going on.

"What's so funny?" I asked.

Both boys roared with laughter. "You're eating a banana like a monkey."

I was peeling the banana halfway down and eating the fruit. The boys then showed me how they would take the peels entirely off before consuming the bananas.

I told them, "My way is better for sanitary reasons."

They countered, "You don't want to look like a monkey, do you?"

Good question.

In the meantime, the rabbits were doing fine, and I had determined I had a male and a female, but I didn't think they were mature enough to breed.

One day, I was curious about the male's weight so I went to the hospital to weigh him on the baby scale there.

Before I could get to the scale, the two girls assigned to the project started beating on the door, "Someone has stolen the male rabbit!"

"Nothing has happened. I have the rabbit in my possession."

They were so relieved, but the damage had already been done. These girls had been frantically searching for the male rabbit for only a few brief minutes, but the word spread through town like a wildfire. All day, I was asked if I had found the male rabbit. Word sure spread in Coari, and everyone seemed concerned about us and what we as Papal Volunteers were doing. Rumors only take minutes to grow, but it seems to take days to quell them.

———————

Ed helped design the chicken house on paper, much like the ones I had seen in Belem. He helped set the timbers for the floor and frame, and the project was off and running. John and Ray were eager to help, and each would come to our aid as time permitted. Raul and Alphonso worked diligently. We had to dig deep holes for the piling so we could attach the chicken house floor to the pilings. Mountains of bamboo had to be gathered to be used for the sidewalls. For the floor, we chose a hardwood that was difficult to saw with a handsaw or drive nails through. In order to smooth one side of the very rough surface of the boards, the boys would use a small but heavy short-handled hoe like a plane. The Brazilians seldom wore anything on their feet other than flip-flops, but when working, they would remove their footwear and use their feet as effectively as their hands. When sawing, for example, they would use their large toe and second toe as a guide for the saw. I often marveled how they didn't cut their toes.

Trying not to let the boys do all the work one day, I took the handsaw and used my forefinger on my left hand as a guide. I pushed down on the saw, only to have the saw take a corner out of my index finger. Blood ran everywhere. I wrapped the finger in a T-shirt and rowed myself to Margaret's hospital across the water. The staff at the hospital couldn't do much more than clean the wound well and professionally dress it by wrapping it really tightly. Whenever I would drop my hand to my side, the finger throbbed with each and every heartbeat, so to ease the throbbing; I held my hand up fairly high whenever I walked.

As I traversed around town and to my canoe to go to the chicken project, Brazilians on the street and those in their houses would come to their door and hold their left hand up in the same position as mine and say, "Hey, Mario!" as if some kind of salute. This continued long after the bandage was gone.

One particular day, the boys; a tall, strapping black man, Pedro; and I were working on the flooring, and as usual for the afternoon, a rain shower came up rapidly. This time, thunder and lightning accompanied the shower. This seldom occurs in Brazil, but this one struck fear in the heart of Pedro. He was holding the hammer, and he suddenly threw it as far away from him as he could. Pedro was a very strong man, and the hammer flew out of sight. I felt we would never find it.

When asked why he did that, he turned toward me with his big eyes bugging out of his head. *"Metalurgia e' relampago!"*

To me, this meant something about lightning and metal or iron. Pedro started to prance around wildly as the two boys doubled over with laughter. The boys explained that Pedro was very superstitious and believed in unseen spirits. Even though the storm was still miles off, Pedro was done for the day as he ran over the hill to his home. The boys told me that Pedro frequented the spiritual dances that often occurred at the river's edge. Séances were often held deep into the night, where a sort of sorcery/spiritualist/witch doctor would call on various mysterious spirits to bring about some source of healing or for other requests. The sick often used this practice instead of going to the hospital at the first sign of symptoms of any ailment. This was one of the main things that the hospital was up against in Coari. When the sick person finally did seek help at the hospital, he was usually very near death. So when the person died in the hospital, it reinforced the notion that the hospital couldn't help the sick people.

The believers of voodoo often wore a symbol (*figa*) that showed their belief in a spiritual power. The sign or image was of a hand with the thumb protruding between the first and index finger. Even while attending Mass in church, it was common to see someone going to Mass and Communion with this symbol hanging around his neck. These people wanted to keep both bases covered. It drove the fathers mad because spiritualism was not considered to be a very religious or educated way of handling things.

Letter to Home
August 6, 1965

Hello, everyone. Some letters did arrive yesterday, and it sure was good to get them. I was getting pretty worried and lonely, but now I feel better. We hope to finish the chicken house tomorrow and move all the chickens over to it. These chickens have been living in the foyer of our house since July 7, which is close to a month. As Margaret put it, "I'll sure be glad when you get those chickens out of here because the whole house smells of chicken poop!" She is right, of course, and I'll be glad too, for then I won't have to clean up after them so much. These chickens are thirty-seven days old, and some weigh over a pound already. Some of the locals cannot believe how fast they grew. One pound is nearly all their adult chickens weigh, and they stand six inches taller. To give you an idea what people know about hybrid chickens, one person said, "When you hatch chickens in a machine, it only takes twenty-four hours for them to hatch." So you can tell some people act like they know a lot, but, again, maybe not. Keep those wonderful letters coming for they really help to stave off homesickness. Sending all of my love, Marvin

---

I overcame the problem of the water separating Coari and the chicken project by buying a sturdy canoe. I purchased one that was deep and firmly made because I couldn't afford to flip over in the lagoon with my heavy work boots. I also didn't know how to swim. For the Brazilians, swimming and falling into the water were second nature to them. For the most part, they could swim like fish at a very tender age. I equated the Brazilians' ability in the water as to Americans being able to ride bicycles. Very few Brazilians in the interior could ride a bike because they never had one or one to borrow. But they were in the water a good percentage of time. During their youth, they were swimming so being in the water wasn't a big deal. I grew up in Iowa where, in my youth, time in the water was rare.

Finally, the chickens were on the project site and out of Margaret's hair and home. We must have made quite a sight moving the chickens over. Each chicken was close to a pound, and there were a hundred chickens to be moved. To do this, we tied four of the chickens' feet together. We each took two sets to the canoe until we had twenty-four. This method took four trips, and we must have made quite a sight for the locals. Once that was done, all the chickens grew quickly, and Raul and Alphonso dug right into the chores. I could rely on them to feed and water the chickens regularly. To feed the chickens, the boys split large bamboo stalks in half and hollowed out the dividers in the center, leaving the end with the natural dividers. A cross bamboo was lashed to each end of the trough to prevent it from rolling over. Watering was another problem due to the round, flat dishes that sat on the floor. Every chicken would take its turn to stand right in the middle of the dish and produce some dropping or calmly sit down in the water to cool off, leaving some residue to pollute the water. Needless to say, keeping the water clean for a long period of time was difficult. The solution to the problem came to me when I remembered my days back on the farm in Iowa. When I was young, I helped my mother raise chickens. One of my duties, among others, was to fill the chicken water receptacle with water. Within a short time, I learned the principle of the watering device, and this concept stuck with me. Now, as I remembered it, was the time to apply it to this situation. As these were the first hybrid chickens in town, things such a feeding or water devices were unheard of. Having someone make one for us would be nearly impossible.

Fortunately, a tin shop was nearby so Raul, Alphonso, and I made our way over there. The tin shop was a small, cluttered place equipped with various tools for cutting tin, a vise, soldering material, and various types of torches. Among other projects and orders, the two men there were making brand-new, never-used, five-gallon cans that were designed to transport kerosene that people used in their lamps and refrigerators. Many people today have no idea that refrigerators could be run solely on kerosene, which we did in our house in Coari because of the few precious hours there was electricity. With the help of Alphonso and Raul, I was able to convey the principle of the chicken water device to the workers. We soon had just what we needed. My idea was to have the water tray high enough on the outside of the can to seal off air getting into the can. This would allow more water to come out until the water level got low enough to allow more water out of the can when the can was tipped over.

Word soon spread that I was a genius, but the idea came from something I had observed as a small boy. My genius didn't do this. It was my exposure to many different things that these Brazilian people hadn't had a chance to experience. With the new self-feed watering device, water was available to the chickens twenty-four hours a day instead of the dirty water that had to be changed every hour or so.

Chicken feed was hard to come by in Coari since everything had to come in by boat and from a good distance. The feed consumption had to be monitored very carefully. Even then, when the order was placed in plenty of time, the boat would sometimes come back from Manaus without any feed. One also had to be careful not to buy too much and have to store the feed because the humidity would permeate the burlap bags, resulting in mold. Feeding moldy feed would create problems and could kill the chickens.

Another problem was that the price of everything was subject to availability. When the suppliers would run low, the price would skyrocket, jeopardizing the project's profitability. When we did run out of chicken mash, we would buy ear corn, shell it by hand, and smash the kernel with a hammer, pulverizing the kernels into the size that the chickens could handle. We could have purchased shelled corn, but the risk of getting moldy corn was also very great. So you could imagine my dismay when the feed consumption of the chickens escalated to double within a week's time. In checking with the boys, they said they had been filling the bamboo troughs completely full at night just before dark so that, when the chickens got up early, there would be plenty of food. The boys felt the plan must have been working because, each and every morning, all the feeders were empty. Not even a crumb was to be found in the bamboo trays. But the project couldn't afford to feed the chickens with this amount of feed consumption. I was sure something was wrong for there was no way the chickens could be eating so much at this stage of growth.

So I decided to check on the chickens across the water one night. The moon was full and high, and I didn't need a lantern or flashlight, even though I had one along. I paddled my canoe across the lagoon, and I made my way up the steep hill to the chicken house. I shined my light through the slats of the chicken house and observed that the boys did a good job with their chores because I could see the bamboo trough filled high with cracked corn.

Satisfied, I started back to the canoe, but something told me to go back and have another look. When I entered the chicken house, I shined the flashlight all around, up above and on the walls. When the beam played across the floor, I spotted this yellow ribbon like mass moving away from the feeder. Right beside it was a red line that seemed to be flowing toward the chicken feed. Once again, I was facing an ant horde that was capable of carrying off and devouring all the chicken project's profits. I stepped outside to see where these fierce hordes of ants were coming from. It wasn't long before I spotted the yellow line heading right for this sizeable hole in the ground about fifty yards from the chicken house. A yellow line was going into the entrance in the ground. A red line was coming out and headed right for the chicken house. Again, these creatures had clearly completed their preparation for running off with the loot. The yellow line of the trail was perfectly cleared and a little wider than the smoothed red trail. I couldn't do much that night because I wasn't going to take on legions of the trap-jaw ants.

The next morning, I was up early and waited for Raul and Alphonso to arrive so I could give them new feeding instructions. My plan was not to put any feed in the feeders in the late afternoon or evening and let the chickens retire hungry. We could fill the trough in the morning, and with that plan, the chickens were a lot more interested in seeing us first thing in the morning. Chicken feed consumption dropped in half, and the chickens showed no signs of slowing in growth.

Remembering the self-feed feeders at home, I drew up a design of one and headed off to the tin shop once again. The tin workers did a marvelous job with my design. Within a week, the self-feeder was hanging six inches off the ground, no longer an obtainable target for the night marauders. Again, the design included one of the five-gallon kerosene cans with several large, square holes cut into it. A tin tray was mounted around the outside of the can. The tray protruded out about two inches and was three inches deep. The top of the can had a six-inch opening, allowing for feed to be poured in. When the chickens consumed a certain amount of feed, more feed would cascade into the tray. Feed consumption stabilized, and the chickens had access to feed anytime. The chickens could no longer waste feed by scratching in it or pooping in the troughs.

Ants were a big problem in Brazil. I once stood under a huge tree for shade and realized that half-moon snippets of leaves were gently raining down on me. Upon closer investigation, I noted a wide, red band of army ants were advancing up the tree trunk. When these ants were up in the tree, they scattered in all directions. When they chanced upon a leaf, they would cut a half-moon fragment out of it. When the leaf fragment fluttered to the ground, other ants would be waiting. The ants would raise the partial leaf in a vertical position. Half-balancing and half-running, the ants formed another column back to the swarm's home deep in the ground. I was told that the ants did this type of cutting of tree leaves at only a particular time of the year and it would not harm the tree.

On one occasion, I was crossing the lagoon in my canoe and noticed what appeared to be red plant leaves jutting out of the water at various locations. I had crossed the lagoon many times and hadn't noticed these red plants being there in the water. I wasn't too far from shore so I turned the canoe around and paddled back to shore to retrieve my camera. When I got back into the canoe, I paddled out to the red plants in the water. When I neared the first one, I saw that the red part of the plants were red fire ants clinging to the plant in huge clusters. Apparently, when the seasonal rains came, the ants became stranded as the water rose around them, leaving them with only one way to go, to climb the fernlike plants. Deeply engrossed in taking pictures at the front of the boat, I failed to realize that the back of the boat was snagged on a rather large clump of ferns that was also loaded with fire ants. Let me tell you that the fire ants didn't intend to share a ride in the boat, and when I realized they had gotten in, I got out. Hoards of ants quickly boarded the boat, and within seconds, angry ants were canvassing the boat. Luckily, I hadn't gone out too far and was able to jump into the water, boots and all. I walked the boat back to shore by holding the rope under water, thereby avoiding the ants from climbing the rope. When I got to shore, I left the boat alone for an hour, and when I returned, not an ant was aboard. I was grateful they had all gone, and I bet they were too.

Chiggers were also very plentiful in the short grass where the jungle had been cleared. The little insects were nearly invisible to the naked eye, and they would embed themselves into my flesh. All of the time I was in Coari, I had terrible raw sores where my socks came out of my boots and especially the whole area around my belt. Every night before taking a shower, I would take a washcloth soaked in rubbing alcohol and scrub my ankles, legs, waist, and private parts in an attempt to kill the insects before they could embed themselves. It seemed to help a little, but applying the alcohol wasn't a picnic either. The only time the problem would ease was if I stayed away from grassy areas for a period of time.

Letter to Home
August 10, 1965

Hello to everyone in Iowa. That picture you sent me of my dog Duke sure brings back the homesickness, and you are right. He takes a good picture. I forgot what a healthy dog looks like for all the dogs down here are in terrible shape. Most of the dogs are just skin and bones, and their hide is covered with mange and lice. Their coats are covered with sores that are continually oozing so no one ever wants to pet them. The poor creatures are left to fend for themselves, and the scraps the locals provide them with are so meager that the dogs spend their days searching for food and continually scratching themselves and licking their sores. No one would think of the humane thing, taking them out of their misery, so they are left to their misery. The mail continues to be slow, and every time the plane lands, I head to the post office, and I camp out, waiting for the mail to be sorted. The personnel at the post office knew why I am there, and they will do their best to quickly sort out the letters for the Volunteers. Some days, I get several. Then there are the terrible days when I wouldn't get any. You letters mean so much to me, and they keep me going. Keep them coming. Love, Marvin

---

There was trouble in paradise. I noticed that all of our chickens were developing watery eyes and watery blisters on their combs. Raul and Alphonso were just sick with worry for they had been doing such a great job of caring for the chickens. Superstition ran wild down here, and the boys were worried that some kind of curse had been placed upon them.

At first, I thought the chickens had come down with a cold or something from being moved too quickly or something. When I scanned my poultry book I had brought from the United States, I found that these chickens were afflicted with a type of chicken pox. Getting a vaccination there was like searching for an air-conditioner or finding an oil well so I resorted to the next best thing, consulting the locals. Sure enough, they had a name for it, *Gogo*. I had no idea what it meant, but I got all kinds of advice. Some suggested applying lemon juice to scratching the combs with a corncob. All of those I consulted seemed to be saying something to the effect of opening the blisters on the comb and getting the blisters to drain. I got some iodine from Margaret at the hospital, and with the boys' help, we opened the blisters and applied iodine blended with penicillin designed for humans and some lemon juice mixed in. In the meantime, I tried to order a remedy from a supplier in Manaus, if they had any idea on what to use. The chickens sure hated the treatment, but I prayed that it worked. I hated the thought of losing any of them.

(In the meantime, the rabbits were nearly six months old, and we planned to breed the doe fairly soon. Lucia and Francesca were doing a wonderful job, and I knew they would take good care of the rabbits as I concentrated on the chickens. I was just sick with worry for the chickens.)

I had been concerned about the water we were using for watering the chickens because the water was being drawn out of the river. The water purity might have had something to do with the pox. I often noted that the local people would come down to the water's edge with a huge pile of laundry, perch themselves on a small wooden platform directly above the water, and do their laundry. The locals worked the soap into the wet clothes, and then they spread the clothes on the platform and beat on them with a wooden paddle, turning the clothes at different intervals. The rinsing process was done the same way. As in both processes, soap would drip back into the river. The unbelievable part of the process was that, when they were finished doing their laundry, they would dip a container in the river and retrieve water to carry back to their home to be used for drinking and cooking. The water's edge also seemed to be a place to dispose of most anything unwanted, which only added to the water pollution. So it wasn't any wonder that I wanted to do something about the source of water being used for the chickens and maybe do something for the purity of the water that humans consumed.

Letter to My Twin Brother, Darwin

August 13, 1965

Hello, Darwin. Thank you for your letter even though I wish you had better news. I was so very shocked and devastated to learn that my best friend from school, Pat, had been killed in a senseless car accident. How awful for his mother, and she had been through so much. When I read your letter, I just lay back on my bed and wept, but no tears would come. Then it came back to me that, one night in a dream, I dreamt my friend had been killed, and it was terrifying. The next morning, I just discounted the dream. I've had many wild dreams since I've been down here, so I just shrugged it off. About three days later, I got this annoying feeling that I should be writing Pat for I owed him a letter. As soon as I thought about writing him, this thought flashed in my mind, "I can't for he has been killed," but I shook myself back to reality, thinking the flash stemmed from the fact of one of my dreams. At any rate, I did pen Pat the letter I owed him, and now I realize he will never get to read it. I feel terrible, and I will pray he is heaven and at peace. I will have a Mass offered by one of the fathers here, and I will write his mother when I know when the Mass is for sure. I know this wasn't an easy letter for you to write, and I thank you for it. I am kind of lost for words right now, and please offer a prayer for Pat as I will from down here. If you learn more about the circumstances, please let me know. Your loving twin brother, Marvin

With a heavy heart, I thought back to my high school days and the wonderful times that we had shared together. Pat was three years younger than I was, but he was my first real friend. When I would come to his house after our Boy Scout meetings, Helen, his mother, was always so nice, and I enjoyed visiting with her. Many times, I would chat with her while she was working at the post office in my hometown, and I knew she felt I was a good influence on her son. What I missed the most was that I was in Brazil, thousands of miles away from home, and I never got to attend the funeral to say good-bye to my friend or console his mother. Janet, his sister, had been in my class, and I wanted to tell her how I felt about Pat and our loss.

My brother's letter to me started, "You know Marvin that the Lord gives and he takes away . . ." With these words, I first thought that something had happened to my dog Duke. For a very brief moment, I was relieved it wasn't that. But when I realized what really had happened, I felt very guilty. I remembered the long letter I had just mailed to him, and I felt terrible that his mother would be the one reading it and possibly renewing her pain. Later, I learned the letter had arrived several weeks after Pat's funeral, and that bothered me all the more.

Shortly thereafter, the chickens were showing signs of responding to our varied treatments. We had changed their treatment to swabbing their combs with disinfectant solution and dabbing their eyes with liquid penicillin. I knew the chickens were especially grateful that we discontinued using lemon juice and corncob brushing as well. I wrote to one of the Redemptorist Brothers in Manaus, who was in charge of supplies, hoping he knew what to use, but I heard nothing.

By September 1, the chickens were doing much better, and it appeared the plague had passed. The only aftereffect appeared to be the many scars on their ruby red combs. I was then able to go ahead with plans for building two more chicken houses in the upcoming months.

We continued to be plagued with the problem of getting water for the chickens because, at the time, we were getting buckets of water directly out of the nearby lagoon. I suspected that might have had a bearing on the health of the chickens. One solution was to dig our own deep well right near the water's edge. We would then draw out seep water, thinking the clay and sand would filter the water to some degree, making the water a little more wholesome. If all went well, the locals would be able to draw much cleaner water than what was found in the lagoon. That would be a boon to all users, especially in the dry season.

Ed, with his expertise in construction, again came to my rescue and helped me design a plan to dig a well on the other side of the lagoon, close to the chicken house. It was also close enough so the inhabitants could use the well. Ray and John offered to help us when they could.

First, we dug a hole seven feet across in circumference and twenty feet deep, thinking we would be going past the water level and clean water would seep into the main shaft. After we dug deep enough, we devised a winch to lower a bucket into the shaft of the well and have someone in the well fill the buckets with dirt. We would winch up the bucket to be emptied. Getting into the well and getting out was completed in the same way, by being lowered or winched up. Each of those involved would dig for an hour and then come up and run the winch for an hour. When one first got lowered into the deepening shaft, it felt cool and a nice place to be, but that feeling quickly passed as one toiled in the pit. The soil was made up of red clay with beige streaks running through the clay. It took a pretty sharp shovel to be able to sink it into the clay without having to stamp or jump on the shovel's edge to get a decent bite of clay. Those wearing heavy boots performed most of this work for one would have to stamp and jump on the spade's bit to make any progress. When the Brazilians worked, they would use a tool similar to a pickax to loosen the clay first.

The first day, we achieved a ten-foot depth and had great plans to complete most of the remaining ten feet the next day. I never knew so many muscles could hurt at the same time as we headed back to the other side of the water where a warm shower and evening meal beckoned.

The second day went as planned, but we only got down another six feet, due to the added difficulty and depth to retrieve the buckets of dirt and the fact that each shovelful was saturated with water. By the second night, I could hardly walk or move, but I headed home with the thought that we would be able to finish by the next day. I could barely paddle the canoe as I was so sore.

When the next morning came, we headed back to the well site, and when we removed our temporary cover from the well, we were aghast to see that the well was over halfway filled with water. During the evening, the seep water crept in like we thought it would, but we hadn't planned for this to happen so soon and at this depth. We started to bail out the water, and it took a long time. When we got most of the water out so we could work, we discovered another problem. Where the clay soil touched the water in the well, the clay collapsed into the well pit, forming a cavity much like an upside-down mushroom, partially filling the shaft back up again with red clay. It was still spreading that morning. It was obviously no longer safe to descend into the well. We should have been more prepared to shore the wall of the well with boards or concrete blocks and complete this as we worked our way down. We knew we had a potential safety hazard lurking there, so the only one thing left to do was fill the hole back in again. It was decided that, if we would attempt this again, we would have cinder blocks or boards ready to act when the time came. Here I was, facing another project failure.

It was fun and interesting to interact with people in the community. I was always surprised that I could find that almost everyone reminded me of a special someone back home. In other words, when I was interacting with the grain dealer for chicken food, this person reminded me of a man who ran the local Clover Farm grocery store in my small hometown in Larchwood, Iowa. Sometimes, the simulation or my perception was not in looks alone, but could be in some of the cases. I concluded that people were human and the same everywhere, no matter where everyone went. Consequently, I made a strong effort to treat everyone as my neighbor.

———————

Brazil would deal with mental illness the way it must have been handled in the United States 150 years ago. I would often pass this particular shack in the back of one person's yard, and I would hear the most hideous moans, groans, panting, and pacing of something or someone caged in a fortified shack. It was very frightening to approach the fence and to peer into the enclosure and try to figure out if the noises were coming from man or beast. It looked like a person as I could only get fleeting glimpses of something moving behind the very narrow slats. Not letting it rest, I told Margaret about what I had heard and seen, hoping she could do something about this. Margaret said she had also heard it and felt maybe it was someone who was mentally unbalanced and perhaps a risk to those around him. I also told Padres Marcus and Jamie, and they agreed they would check it out. A couple weeks went by before I passed that way again. As I approached the very same place, there were no moans, grunts, or pacing as in the past. I peered through the fence, and to my surprise, the shed/cage door was ajar, obviously empty. It stayed empty for all the time I continued to pass by. When I queried about that building and its occupant, no one knew anything.

On another occasion, I was walking down this long, sloping hill across the main plaza of town when I heard and saw this commotion of many young people chasing and taunting this man with sticks, stones, and shouts. The man was running as fast as he could, and he was trying his best to get away from the band of mean people. The appalling part was that shopkeepers and bystanders were observing these groups of kids. Instead of trying to prevent the happenings, the adults seemed to be cheering them along, especially when a rock or stick found its mark. I couldn't believe what was happening as I watched the fleeing person circle the plaza. I could see he was panting and tiring to a slow stumble. I stepped into the man's path, turned, and yelled at the kids to leave and disband and to leave this man alone, which they did grudgingly. The man looked me in the eyes. I could see his eyes were wild with fear. Rivulets of sweat covered his face, and he was panting so hard that I thought he was going to collapse. He smelled as if he hadn't bathed in years. He just continued his wild stare, as I tried to speak to him in very simple phrases and one-word sentences, but to no avail. When I ascertained it was safe for the man, I continued on my way to my house because it was dinnertime. I hoped the man would continue on his way, but no such luck. He kept pace with my every step as he looked about warily.

When I got to the house, I quickly slipped in the door by squeezing through the narrowest of opening. I gestured for him to stay put and promised I would get him something to eat. When I returned with a small sandwich and a cupful of rice, the man grabbed it hungrily.

I probably won't see him again as he's off to the jungle's edge at a swift pace.

I was wrong. Whenever I would walk across the plaza, he'd come at a dead run right at me, to where I thought he would knock me down. The man would then walk with me until I got to the other side of the plaza. This man never seemed to be bound for any particular place. This ritual went on every day for the next several weeks, and then suddenly he was gone. I never saw him again. I thought the man had a limited mentality, but shopkeepers and other Brazilians said he was from an Indian tribe in the interior. Perhaps his tribe had ousted him and he had to set out on his own. Whatever the case was, I still couldn't expel this experience from my mind, how parents and grown adults could stand by and even cheer on inhumane treatment of a lesser capable human being. I had heard that the Indian tribes in the interior were considered fair game, and when the locals were hunting in the jungle, it wasn't wrong to shoot these Indians on sight. I had never really believed this could be happening until after this incident. I was now not so sure.

The young ladies of Coari were beautiful to behold for, on the most part, every woman had a great figure because of all the physical exercise she would get just to survive. There wasn't any transportation to carry them anywhere, and everything had to be done physically. Wash day meant carrying the heavy laundry down to the river's edge where the soiled clothing was pounded repeatedly to get them clean and then rinsed in the river water. The wet laundry was then loaded back into the basket and carried on their head back to their residence. Oftentimes, they would carry a large pail of water along as well. Going to the market usually meant a long walk to its location and then carrying their purchases back to where they lived. There were no strollers to carry babies or carts to transport items. When transporting something heavy, they would balance the parcel on their heads and walk very erect. Oftentimes, one would approach a curvaceous figure from behind and couldn't help but admire the fine creature walking ahead. But all thoughts of fancy would be dashed to pieces because, when she would turn and smile, invariably, decaying teeth would fill her mouth. Tooth decay was a major problem for these people from infancy on. Many were on a steady diet of some source of sugar, cane sugar, bananas, and other naturally sweetened foods. As babies, they were spoon-fed smashed bananas instead of cereals as we did in the United States. Oral hygiene was practically nonexistent in the interior, and it would be years before it would became available. I was told that the problem was so severe that women wouldn't consider leaving the interior to go to modern cities due to the condition of their teeth.

The men also had very strong physiques from doing very difficult tasks manually, such as unloading freight from boats that came in fifty-kilogram burlap bags, equivalent to or in excess of one hundred pounds. In construction, everything was carried in buckets on top of their heads, such as sand, cement, water, and bricks. Oral hygiene was also a problem for the men. But to me, the appearance of the condition of men and their mouth didn't seem as shocking.

One very outgoing girl in particular, Tecca, must have been in her mid-teens. She used to just love to stand and look into the Papal Volunteers eyes that were blue, which were seldom seen in the interior of Brazil. Tecca would make any excuse to stop us on the street and pretend to have something important to say while she and her friends would just stare into our eyes.

They would often mutter, "*Oleos lindo!*"[14]

It got difficult at times to avoid Tecca and her team of teenage girls. When I did see them, I would run for my house, dive in, slam the door, and hide behind it, but undaunted Tecca would call through the door with giggles and words of love.

---

[14]   Beautiful eyes

Everyone in the house would tease me unrelentingly about Tecca and her pursuit of us younger Papal Volunteers. Several times, Ray and I would watch the leisurely pace of Coari from our second-story bedroom window with Tecca usually lurking about. Ray would call out her name and duck down real quickly when he saw her. There I would be just flat-footed and shocked, and she would turn and see me standing there with a stupid look on my face. I knew she thought that I wanted her. If Ed were a witness, he would just lose it laughing because he had often witnessed me racing home to slam the door on Tecca's hot pursuit.

Ed would say, "Here comes Mario on the run with the feeling of Tecca's hot breath on the back of his neck." Then Ed would slap his knee in loud laughter.

On one occasion, Ray talked me into going to a local school dance just to spend time and observe the happenings. On that particular evening, Tecca exploded across the room, grabbed me for a dance, and pulled me out onto the dance floor. I had never danced so close and erotic before in my life. The more I struggled to get away, the more Tecca pulled me in closer. When the dance was over, I bolted for the door and ran home with Ray close at my heels. After all, he didn't want to be left alone with Tecca and her team because he had blue eyes as well.

Once again, Ed came to the rescue with this sage advice, "Mario, Tecca is like a dog chasing a car. If the dog ever catches the car, the dog wouldn't know what to do with it. Slow down a little, look her right in the eyes, and tell her you are in love with her. Then she will be stopped in her tracks, and she will be like you and run the other way."

It took a lot of tall talking to convince me of this, but something had to be done because Tecca was growing bolder and would stand below my open window to yell, "Mario, I love you!" in very broken English. She was starting to zone in on my daily pattern because she would be a lot closer to head me off when I made my dash for the house.

Finally, I had it and worked up enough courage to take Ed's advice. One day as I sauntered for the house, Tecca bolted out of the shadows and ran full speed at an angle to cut me off midway in the plaza. I continued my sauntering pace, and it took all of the courage I could muster as Tecca adjusted her angle of interception and zeroed in on me.

When she got close, I called out to her, "*Tecca minha amora!*"[15]

The look on Tecca's face was priceless as she jerked to a stop and I advanced toward her, reaching out as if I wanted to hug and squeeze her. As I advanced, she retreated, puzzled as to the sudden change. The closer I pretended I wanted to be, the further she wanted to get away. After that, Tecca was no longer a threat or problem to me, but the aggression on her part shifted to Ray, and he eventually had to employ the very same tactics. Dating the Brazilians was not encouraged for the Papal Volunteers, and I didn't intend to do it because it would have been a distraction to my real mission in Brazil.

———————

There wasn't a lot of industry in Coari, but one exception was the brick factory that made red clay bricks for building clay brick structures. Eventually, the town mustered enough money to start paving the main thoroughfare in town. Red clay bricks were laid on their side. A very thin layer of cement was poured over the bricks to smooth over the surface and hold the bricks in place on the road. After the first street was completed, through some political moneys promised to the city, a large flatbed truck was shipped in by boat. The truck belonged to the city, and drivers who knew nothing about the rules of driving handled it. They would often speed down the one street at a high rate of speed, putting everyone and everything in jeopardy that was in their path. When the truck had completed its one block of smooth driving, speed was no longer an issue because of the huge ruts in the rest of the town's dirt streets. This forced the crazed drivers to slow to a crawl speed, and if they didn't, they were at risk of being thrown from the driver's seat. The city truck was used for some hauling, but mostly its main purpose was to transport loads of workers to and from city projects.

After a second street on the main thoroughfare was completed, the city acquired a Volkswagen Combie van that was equipped as an ambulance for the hospital to use. The second day after the ambulance had arrived in the town, the ambulance experienced a head-on collision with the town's truck, luckily without too much damage. The drivers of each vehicle had

---

[15]   Tecca, my love!

no idea on which side of the road to operate, and as the two vehicles bore down on each other, the driver of each vehicle panicked and couldn't find the brake in time before they collided.

Ray and I were once asked to take the ambulance to meet the airplane that was due to land in the water very soon. Ray opted to drive, and he had to drive at a very slow rate across the rutted turf to the water's edge. There we waited while a very ill passenger, who was near death from a snakebite, was carefully helped from the airplane into a boat and brought to shore. We removed the stretcher from the ambulance and arranged the blanket that was on top of the stretcher across its length. We then helped the man onto the stretcher. He was very weak and clearly in lot of pain as his left foot was so swollen that the foot had split open between his toes. As we drove slowly back to the hospital, the patient would moan and cry out with every bump and rut we encountered. Fearing the worst that this man was very near death, Ray drove even faster and hit all the bumps harder. The man screamed out in more pain the faster we went. Finally arriving to the hospital, we helped to carry the stretcher into the hospital and placed the man in a bed. He seemed to be better already as he had stopped his groaning and laid back into the bed. When Ray and I loaded the stretcher back into the ambulance, I noticed we had failed to swing the brace for the front legs of the stretcher back under the stretcher. The brace that wasn't supposed to be there was lying across the stretcher bed. This tall, sharp, flat piece of steel was protruding into the man's back, and it must have been very painful. It was no wonder he was moaning and groaning with each bump. The man eventually survived and, for some reason, declined an ambulance ride back to the plane when he returned home.

———

At last, the chickens were completely over the fowl pox. All in all, they survived it fairly well for we lost only three. We finally heard from the Brazilian government, and they advised it was better to refrain from vaccinating and letting the chickens develop their own immunity. If one would start vaccinating the chickens, then it would have to be repeated every six months or so. The same would go for all the new hatches. We knew this wouldn't work well with the intention of getting these chickens out to the locals, and the follow-up would be very difficult. At this stage, we could only trust the advice given and see what happened.

Construction on the second chicken house had begun, and it was intended to be a laying house for hens. Work was urgent, as it wouldn't be too long before some of the pullets would start to do their thing. This building was twenty-six feet long and fourteen feet wide, about the same height as the last building. The joke among the Papal Volunteers was that I wanted to stay in compliance with the zoning commission, which, in reality, there was no such thing. Future plans included building a much smaller structure to be used as a brooder house. All three of these building were sitting on the fathers' land. Raul and Alphonso couldn't believe where I got all these ideas because, for them, they thought we had already surpassed all expectations. Looking back, I probably would have handled it a bit differently for the boys were beginning to believe there would never be any money in it for them.

The water level by this time was way down from the previous level in the lagoon. This season was locally called the "ugly season" because the water, what there was, was usually trapped in the lagoon. The water would turn quite stagnant. Many people would get more severe stomach problems from drinking this water. This season kept Margaret very busy, and I really wished my well project would have gone differently.

———— ·—————

One of John's many duties was to help Padre Marcus with the Food for Caritas program. Food would be shipped down to Coari in large fifty-five-gallon drums and was to be distributed to the poor through the Redemptorist parish in Coari. John was, at times, at odds with the fathers on how the distribution was handled. To John, it seemed that sometimes the food and clothing in the program was used for payment of services rendered to the fathers as part of wages granted. It was a tough call.

I once helped John hand out some of the clothing that had just arrived. Many people lined up in a long line as the word spread. I watched as he handed out this particular tie-dyed shirt, among other things, to this apparently poor mother. To my surprise, a few days later, I noticed this young boy flying a kite. The same tie-dyed shirt had been torn up and used in the kite's construction. I mentioned this to Padre Marcus.

"That is why you will sometimes be disappointed in the value placed on something if it is just handed out. If that person who received the shirt had to earn it, then the shirt would have never ended up as a scrap of material used as a kite."

I could see his point.

Another problem John had to overcome was the use of food that was shipped to Coari. The problem was in the type of food that was shipped in the drums. It usually consisted of a very fine ground cornmeal and dried powdered milk, which the Brazilians had no concept of what it was or how to use it. John was in charge of the project. He had a very good command of the language and worked tirelessly at solving these issues. John and Margaret worked together in raising the nutritional level of the very poor.

About the same time, two large burlap bags of chicken feed/mash arrived from Manaus, and was it ever welcome. We had run entirely out of mash the week before so we had to resort to the finely ground cornmeal sent down through the charity system. The fathers had received several fifty-five-gallon drums of a very fine ground cornmeal that was intended to feed the poor and hungry of Coari. We at the chicken project took the ground cornmeal and mixed it with some ground wheat from the local miller and dried milk from the Caritas program. The chickens had the same reaction as the locals, but they had to eat something. We supplemented the chicken's daily ration with some grass that we harvested by hand. Now that the new shipment of feed was in, we continued to mix in some of the finely ground cornmeal that nobody seemed to want with the new mash. This made the feed last longer in order to try to maintain some sort of diet without all the fluctuations. I bet some people in the United States would have blown their tops if they knew we were dipping into the food for charity program and feeding it to chickens.

———

Politics were always alive and well in Brazil, and in Coari, there was no exception. On one occasion, several years previously, someone running for a political position had promised an airport for the city of Coari and had actually cleared a road for five miles out into the jungle. The project even got as far as seven acres of land had been cleared for the airport. To keep the jungle from creeping back, a type of elephant grass, which I recognized from Santarem, had been planted on the seven-acre site. As what usually happened, once that person got into office, all work toward the promised prize ceased. Not unlike any other city in Brazil, Coari was full of many half-completed projects. For a new politician to finish someone else's project would have been unheard of.

Among some of the things promised to me while I was still in the States was that I would have use of a tractor and farm equipment. After arriving in Coari, I found out that the tractor was the only source of power to run the city's generator, so it couldn't stray too far or too long from the generator. The farm equipment that was promised included a disc or, as some people called it, a harrow. When I inspected the disc/harrow, I learned it had been brought to Coari during WWII and the disc was left with its plates into the ground. After twenty years, rust had taken its toll, for the bottom half of the blades was nearly rusted off while the top half was in fairly good shape. So one Sunday, Ray and I decided to walk to the proposed site of the airport landing strip. We thought we could walk the eight kilometers and be back in time for our noon meal. What fools we were for we really had to step it off. The heat was very oppressive, and the road was very hilly. We barely made it out there and back by sunset. I did see a real possibility for a future project. With the elephant grass growing there and keeping the jungle at bay so far, I knew I had time to develop my idea.

Ray and I learned on our hike to the airport that this was a good place to start if one had the desire to head out into the jungle because, the further out, the more wild the jungle would be. So one day, John, Ed, Ray, and I decided to go on a safari into the jungle to pursue wild boar and hunt whatever else would cross our paths. We didn't want to go to deep into the jungle without a guide so Alphonsos older brother, Pedro, volunteered. Pedro had been our guide before when we went into the jungle to retrieve building supplies so I felt reasonably confident that he could do the job. I later learned that one could approach most any male in the town of Coari and that person would boast of his ability to conduct a tour of the jungle.

After much preparation and planning, early one morning, Ray, John, Ed, Pedro, and I hitched a ride on the city truck that was going out toward the airport site. At the end of the road, we hopped off and headed in the jungle. We followed one of the many trails that existed close to the end of the road. After some easy going for an hour or so, we veered off the trail and pursued some sounds that sounded like wild pig. I had read about wild boar and related my cautionary probabilities of what could occur and what safety measures we should take if we should encounter them. I had pretty well scared everyone as all were losing their zeal of pursuing such creatures. Not heeding distance or direction, we plunged forward in the tangled jungle, always heading toward the sound we thought to be grunts and brush movements that wild board caused. The closest we got to the wild boars was fresh droppings, pungent smell of pig, and some trampled foliage on the jungle floor. Flying over the jungle, one does not get the sense of the terrain and how hilly and difficult it is to traverse. Remember, there was no such thing as cell phones or GPS.

Comfortable with Pedro as our guide, we unknowingly were getting quite deep into the jungle, and we were getting away from any trail that would ease our pursuit. While deep into the jungle, we encountered huge termite mounds that exceeded the height and width of a large automobile.

Every now and then, we'd come to a clearing that would allow us to see a few hundred feet or so, and we could look out to some large trees that rimmed the next part of the jungle. There, I spotted a toucan, a large-billed bird. I was armed with Ed's British Enfield 303 army rifle. Anxious to shoot something, I aimed and fired. All of the jungle noises from the birds, insects, and animals came to a dead stillness as if all the creatures were trying to figure out what was going on. The bullet found its mark, and when I went to claim my prey, I could only find its beautiful large beak and two legs still attached by some flesh of its tail. I felt very guilty for taking the shot, and the other Papal Volunteers weren't too proud of me either.

Ed was carrying a chrome-plated .357 magnum with an elk-horned handle, and when he shot it into a fibrous tree at two different points, a very long board fell from the other side of the tree. With all of our firepower, we had little to show for our trek into the wilds of the jungle. It was nearing noon, and right after we finished our sandwiches, we decided to head back, but where was back? Our guide was no help for he, too, was lost. After a lot of discussion and some logic thrown into the mix, we started to retrace our trail. We found the return seemed to be so much further than how far we had come in pursuit if game.

It was getting toward three o'clock when John pulled up lame with a severe cramp and muscle spasm in his left leg. He was completely immobilized. We all knew the darkness would completely envelop us in another few hours, and even if we got back to the airport road, it still was another five miles back to Coari. We devised a makeshift harness with the aid of our belts and a fresh-cut sapling that we put across John's shoulders and across ours, one on each side, which aided him in walking on one leg. I'm not known for having sympathy for anyone in pain, but I realized how large a man John was and how I felt bad for him and what he was going through. Ed, being the strongest, stayed at his post without being told while Ray, Pedro, and I took turns between helping John and carrying all the gear. It was very slow going at this pace, and we all knew the danger of the darkness. No one wanted to spend the night in the jungle where it got very cold and extremely dark. We grimly trekked on, and after what seemed like days, we finally broke through the jungle wall out onto the airport road. To our surprise and relief, the town truck soon pulled up with its load of workers on its way back to town. It must have taken ten of us to get John up on the flatbed of the truck as darkness closed in. Despite the very bumpy ride, the truck felt like a Cadillac all the way back to town.

———

Back at the chicken project, we were enjoying a successful selling period, and we had some new rules on selling the chickens. We changed the process as we had heard some feedback that some of the locals doubted the moral upbringing of our chickens. I really couldn't blame them, considering the first of these chickens arrived as orphans with no mother hens in sight. Now they were going public without the watchful eye of their father roosters. I devised a new plan to only sell a hen and rooster together. They must go as a couple, and the people buying them had to agree to a verbal contract. They had to accept the fact that these two chickens were already married, so to speak, and they were meant to stay together. Ten sets sold immediately with the new rule, and the project had sold twenty-five roosters before this new plan was put into motion. The local people couldn't believe that these chickens were only three months old because of their size. The buyers were informed that it would take another few months before the couple would produce eggs. At first, we had no reports of diseases or deaths from the ten couples.

My long-range plan included a three-tiered program for getting these hybrid chickens out into the locals' hands. First, the people were urged to purchase a married couple (a hen and rooster) and to raise them in their own setting. Second, the people were told to buy a rooster or hen to mate with its own stock. Third, which was the least expensive and probably the most popular, the people were to purchase a half-dozen eggs from the hybrid hens and take the eggs and hatch them with the old clucks they had in their own backyard. There didn't seem to be a shortage of old clucks around, and some of these old clucks seemed so skinny that I didn't know if they had enough body heat to hatch eggs. The hens from the first batch of chickens were getting close to laying eggs. It was too soon for phase three, but I knew it wouldn't be too long until the project would start to pay off.

Toward the end of September, we had finished the roof on the second chicken house, and it looked really good, even if I say so myself. The roof was made from a special kind of palm-like branches with wide leaves that would all lay flat when attached to hardwood sticks by wrapping them with hemp and attaching them to the rafters with some more of the hemp cord. The locals called this kind of branches *pilha*.[16] Several layers were laid flat, and it did a great job of shedding the heavy rains and, at the same time, allowing the heat out of the building and the sun from getting in. All of this *pilha* had been gathered from the jungle, and we wrapped it. The boys showed me the process, and it did take a little time to acquire the knack. This kind of roof would last two to five years depending on how thick it was applied. We spaced our *pilha* at a minimum due to time and money.

One thing that did slow the project down on the second house was that we had to wait for our order of hardwood planks from the local mill. While we waited, we finished the side of the building with split bamboo and completed the steps and door. We were told we would have to wait until mid-October for the planks, but I went and asked the fathers to get involved in the process. With their influence, the waiting period sped up. That was the way it worked down here. Sometimes, one needs to approach the right person with some influence to help oneself out.

---

[16]   Pile on

About that same time, my people on the rabbit project and I had a meeting early in the morning. We decided that was the day to mate the buck and the doe. Word must have flown around town because, by the time we put the two together, forty or fifty people gathered, expecting a real show. To everyone's disappointment, the buck rabbit spent his together time sniffing and smelling all parts of the cage and totally ignored the female rabbit. Padre Jamie, the priest helping me in all facets of my projects, offered some advice, but the buck wasn't even listening. The young ladies on the rabbit team felt they had let the whole town down, and it occurred to me how word must have gotten out. We decided to try another day and, at that time, only reveal the plan minutes before joining the two rabbits in an attempt not to draw a crowd. It appeared some of the rumors one heard about rabbits might not be true.

To pass the time during the evenings, the Papal Volunteers would often listen to the "Voice of America Radio" to keep abreast of the sports, but when the news came on, there would be invariably a lot of static and jamming, which Cuba allegedly did. Oftentimes, we could only rely on bits and pieces of news straight from the United States in letters or when a visitor would chance through Coari.

The field of grass that Ray and I had seen was five miles out of town, and I kept thinking back to the fact that the land could be used to produce something locally. After talking to Padre Jamie, I realized rice would be the answer because it was already a stable in the Brazilian diet. To my surprise, several varieties of rice could be grown without having to flood the field with water. So while waiting for the chickens to mature, I begged Padre Marcus for the use of the tractor. I planned to use the old disc despite its condition. Padre Marcus finally conceded but warned me that the tractor could only be used after ten in the morning and it had to be back on the generator by four. I agreed, and another project was on. The rice seed was ordered, and upon its arrival, Padre Jamie and I headed out to the site to start the land preparation.

The elephant grass seemed quite similar to the grass Brother Norbert was using in Santarem. It had grown up to eight feet high, and we found it was very difficult to knock it down and work it into the soil with the disc. That wasn't the only problem. When we attempted to pull the disc through the grass, we couldn't see the hazards that were strewn on the ground, namely fallen logs and large holes in the turf. The jungle would produce some wonderful hardwoods, and several such logs were lying in our way as we attempted to clear the field. One particular log was so hard that we ruined two axe blades. It seemed to be petrified wood, but, of course, it was not. Eventually, we decided the log was too large and durable so we decided we'd just have to farm around it. One of the Brazilians called the wood *marsarinduba*. I never did learn what the word meant, but I had heard of it before when used in reference to a wonderful hardwood that was practically indestructible.

I initially had no desire to use the Brazilian method of cutting the grass, and after a few days burning the entire residue off the land, it wouldn't utilize the nutrients in the grass. The more we tried, the more difficult it became. The disc kept knotting up with the tall grass so we had to stop every few feet to untangle the mess. Eventually, we stopped unplugging the disc and left the disc knotted as we drove across the field at different angles in an effort to knock the butter grass down. This took up the first day of the tractor's allotted time as we had to be very cognizant of logs, stumps, large stones, and time.

After waiting a week, Padre Jamie and I took the tractor back out to the site, mainly for transportation, and we proceeded to rake the dry vegetation into clumps, all by hand. We spent a full two days on the raking process, and when completed, we set the heaps of dead grass on fire and did a controlled burn, what the Brazilians had done for years. Throughout the whole process, we were wary of the many insects that lived there, especially the fire ants. We took the disc back over the burned grass and turned the ashes into the soil, a good source of potash for the depleted soil. I really wanted to use another method than burning, but I had no recourse.

The following week, we returned to the field with the rice seed and sowed it by hand, trying not to omit too many large areas. Once the sowing was completed, we went over the entire field again with the disc to work the rice seed into the soil. Rain usually would start around four daily so we often drove the tractor back to Coari in the pounding rain. On the last trip with the tractor, we returned the disc to Coari and parked it where it had stood for the last twenty years.

We were able to get about three acres sowed and worked in with the disc. Then it rained very lightly for thirty-six hours straight, giving the rice a good chance of germinating. We had to wait a few days before we could go out to the field for the dirt road was all muddy. And it was too far to walk five miles in the gooey mud.

When the weather permitted, I would occasionally take the tractor out to the field of rice or hop a ride on the town's truck when I was notified of the workers' departure. And like most first-time farmers, I worried the grain out of the ground. When it did sprout, I found many places that the ants had been busy at work. The good thing was the rice plants grew so fast that, after a certain stage, the ants lost their interest in the rice stalks and started to seek other things that were just sprouting among the rice plants.

Meanwhile, I had received several disturbing letters from my home in Iowa detailing how my dad's landlord was pulling some unethical dealings. My dad had purchased eighty acres from the same landlord and rented another eighty acres from her at a set price. This agreement went on without conflict for ten years or more, but another farmer approached the landlord and offered to buy the same eighty acres at an inflated price. In the rental agreement, my dad had the first option to buy the eighty acres, but the price was higher than the bank would loan my dad so he had no option but to decline the purchase. I was extremely upset as I wrote to my parents.

Marvin J. Schuttloffel

Letter to My Parents
September 24, 1965

Hello, Mom and Dad. I simply couldn't believe the guile and deceit that is going on there at home. How can this be when we have catered to our landlord every time we could? Please try to forgive our landlord for selling the eighty acres of land out from under you and the evils in their hearts. I prayed about it before falling asleep. While I slept, I felt I received the following message. It seems as if God permits some people to do evil things, and these actions only afford us the opportunity to forgive. The road to heaven is strewn with rocks and many crooked bends and only the faithful can and will persevere. In this vision, I was asked to ask you to forgive and pray for the evildoers as God expects us to straighten the path to heaven through prayer. Remember that God is all about forgiveness, and we are not to let him down. In this vision, I told God that, if anything happens, I see no other way than to leave here and come to your aid to help fight the fight. I cannot express how angry and frustrated I am over this. For the first time in my life, I felt I was actually accomplishing something, and I would hate to leave now, but it is in God's hands. I promise I would never keep anything from them, and I hoped they would do the same for me. I feel so powerless to help you while I am so far away, but always remember that we are all together even though miles separate us now. I have been making it to daily Mass every day, and I will be praying hard over this. Please keep me posted. Love, Marvin

---

The next day, I wrote the landlord and poured it on about how hard it was to make progress in Brazil. I enclosed a picture that was hers to keep. I asked her to take it to my folks and show them the picture in the guise of getting her to see my parents. Maybe I hoped the landlord would change her mind on what she was about to do. Looking back, my plan failed for my dad didn't exercise his option to buy the eighty acres of land.

Letter to Home
October 23, 1965

Hello, Mom and Dad. How goes the battle on the home front? Please be sure to keep me posted, and please do not hold anything back. I am really loaded down with work this week and the last. My plan for getting the flooring delivered to the second chicken house site moved along a little faster out of the mill after a well-timed visit from the fathers. Good ol' politics! I am told the four hundred new baby chicks will arrive by airplane tomorrow so we have to hurry and finish the second house and move the remaining laying hens and a few roosters to their new abode. All the Papal Volunteers had a retreat last Thursday, and I hated to take the time, but I asked my team of boys to stay focused on the building of the second chicken house. They did just that. I let the boys know I would be back in time to help get the first house cleaned thoroughly and condense the size of the first building so the chicks stay together. While I was at retreat, I learned the order for the four hundred chickens had been interrupted due to some controversy on the payment. Father Clem held the retreat, and he pulled me aside and suggested I prepare to transfer my several projects to someone else for the Papal Volunteer organization had some other plans for me. Needless to say, I was floored for I had never considered anything else. I love you all, and I miss everyone terribly. I am keeping you in my prayers. Love, Marvin

---

When I had returned to Coari, I was no closer to receiving the four hundred baby chicks that we had ordered. It was probably just as well for the second chicken house still wasn't completed. I knew Margaret would have no part of four hundred chickens in our house this time.

One day shortly after my return, Alphonso cut his ankle with a saw. The cut happened to be right over a blood vein, and he bled profusely. I helped get him to the hospital after finding where to apply pressure to reduce the bleeding. Alphonso was a good patient, and with quick action, I knew he was going to be fine. I told him to stay home and take as long as necessary to heal.

———

The rabbit hutches were close to the hospital. As the two girls were feeding the rabbits one morning, I decided we would immediately attempt to mate the pair. The two girls were breathless as the doe and the buck wasted no time in doing a fine job. I informed them that we had thirty days to get ready for the new additions. I was sure they spread the word on how everyone missed the big show.

Letter to Home
October 7, 1965

Hello, everyone in Iowa. I was so thankful to get your letter from home, and it was such a relief to hear all is well. You will probably never know how I wait and long for your letters. I don't mean to say that you never write by any means, but I want you to know how much those letters from home mean to me. This is no kidding. Sometimes when the plane comes in with the mail, I may have five or six letters, but if none of them is from home, I feel shorted. It sure brought back pleasant memories to hear that the rural route salesman for Raleigh's is still on the road, and it must have been wonderful that he stayed for supper and visited. I vividly remember how ol' Pete Wielenga would carry his big heavy case into the kitchen and start on his pitch right away as he handed out sticks of chewing gum to all of us kids. While presenting his wares, he would open up a bottle and let us take a deep sniff. Then he would raise the bottle up to the light and say, "Look at how much is gone! You sniffed that much?" And then he would laugh and smile a huge toothy grin. As I write this, I can just vision his happy face while he is walking up the sidewalk from his old '48 Chevy panel truck. What a wonderful man, and if fate permits, I would love to see him again. He is indeed a wonderful friend. I remember, too, how Mom would just love to have him visit, and she would always figure out something to buy whether it was carbolic salve or some spices for cooking. Mom would only use the vanilla extract that Pete sold. Is it true that pheasant season is getting close to opening? I remember when we all couldn't wait for the day, and I can still hear my twin brother, Darwin, say when he would miss a shot, "These damn reloaded shells." Oh by the way, when you get this letter, I will have been in Brazil for a year now, which leaves me only two more years to go down here. Love, Marvin

---

By the end of October, it was beginning to be very hot, and we still hadn't received the four hundred baby chicks that were supposed to have arrived two weeks before. It seemed to happen quite often that the first date promised on everything down here wasn't necessarily the actual date that things would happen. I kept hearing, "This is Brazil," as if to say "Don't get into a fuss." To affirm this, we had only gotten half of the wood for the floor of the second chicken house. It was just as well because the new chickens hadn't arrived yet. I was told that, when the plane came in the next day, maybe, just maybe. From the first batch of chickens that we still had left, some of the chickens weighed about four pounds each, and they were only four months old. Nobody around here could believe how fast they had grown.

These four-pound chickens were eating us out of house and home so, while we waited for the rest of the wood, we built a fence between the two chicken houses so the laying hens could go outside and scratch around in the soil and cool off if there were a breeze. The fence consisted of split-in-half bamboo stalk, the very same we used in the sides of the buildings but longer, which made a stockade-type of fence. It worked fairly well. There was an endless supply of bamboo, and it was easy to find. The termites loved the stuff after it dried out, so one must continually keep an eye on it and replace some of the bamboo every three months or so. Several locals had advised me not to keep such beautiful hens from touching the ground, as some of these people had weird ideas on what lurked in the soil. In my travels, I had seen a lot of chickens on the ground, and I was sure there would be no problem. I calculated that it would be a win-win situation with hens on the ground eating ants that were trying to steal their food. Maybe the chickens could supplement their ever-increasing desire for food. The rooster project was going great, and we were in the process of selling some of the roosters. We had sold six more to date. Some of the locals wanted to place the roosters in their backyard, and I was quite concerned about the chickens' welfare for none had ever been on the ground. With the condition of these people's small fenced-in backyards, who knew what was lurking back there? Our plan was to get a few out there for consumption and let the word spread on the quality of meat, thus getting everyone's attention. The long-range plan was to sell the chickens as a couple, one hen and a rooster, but we had to sell some roosters to get some money and some good PR. The plans swirling around in my head included ideas on marketing more roosters in the future and perhaps getting up to four hundred or more chickens. About that time, I told the fathers to steel themselves for more construction projects in the future.

The first set of chickens matured rapidly, and not one Brazilian could pass the chicken house without peeking between the bamboo slats to monitor the chickens' growth. It wasn't long before the boys reported that they were getting some pretty good offers from people who wanted to buy a chicken to eat. I knew this couldn't be if the project were to have a lasting impact on the local community. Even though the cash offers would ease the money coffer's problem, that wasn't the long-term goal, or the vision I had.

In order to reach the goal I had set, I instructed the boys to spread the word that the chickens were nearing adulthood and they would only be sold as a couple, meaning one hen and one rooster. I knew the local people would approve of this arrangement because of their interest in the proper order of the family. After a few days, Alphonso and Raul told me that a lot of people said they couldn't afford two chickens and could only eat one at a time. I realized my intent had been misunderstood, so I sent Raul and Alphonso back out with the message that these chickens weren't to be eaten at all. These chickens were now a married couple, and soon they would start laying eggs. From those eggs would come their family. If one of the couple were eaten, the remaining partner would have a broken heart.

As word spread, so did sales. Fairly soon, we had excess cash. Rather than splitting the money between the two partners, I had to convince them that, as a project, we had to build another chicken house and expand the operation. We couldn't just order more baby chicks and try to raise them in the same chicken house among the adult birds. We needed more separate floor space. So the second chicken house took shape rather quickly with everyone's help, and the second batch of chickens was ordered. How was I to know at the time that I had trouble brewing?

Letter to Home
October 30, 1965

Hello, Mom, Dad, and everyone. I received three letters today, and although it is great to hear from other people, your letters mean the most to me. It isn't that I don't enjoy letters from other people, but the letters from home are much more important. You asked how I spent my first anniversary down here, and I admit I had a few beers and a very good time. I didn't get tipsy, and I didn't have any trouble getting home in the rain. The rain was a very welcome sight, and with it comes cooler weather, at least for a while. Another benefit is that, when it rains, I can stop working outside, and it gives me a chance to get some letter writing done. If I write on a hot day, by the time I get done, a pool of sweat is usually on the floor by my chair. You may think I am kidding, but it's true. The first few times, I couldn't believe I sweated that much, but down here, one sweats all the time and eventually gets used to it. I received a letter from the Holy Cross Brother who is currently in the United States, and he plans to be in Santarem by November 25, and I will plan my vacation around that time and try to connect with Brother Norbert and see him there on the farm. I expect to leave Coari on December 2 and go upriver to see other Papal Volunteers on the way. The four hundred chickens I ordered some time ago haven't arrived yet, and I feared my order and money fell into the wrong hands, but I received a telegram telling me that my order has been delayed. The problem with the word "delay" down here can mean anything from a month to a year. If the order were only going to be delayed a week or so, the producer wouldn't even take the time to write for it is an unwritten law down here that one or two weeks isn't considered anything major. It's like a delay at home of one or two days. Keep those wonderful letters coming, and they are the only thing that keeps me going. Love, Marvin

---

On one particular trip out to see the rice field, I encountered a weathered Brazilian standing in the midst of the field. This man's skin looked like tanned leather, and I could tell this skin color was due to very long exposure in the tropical sun. The grain was standing waist high and showing signs of heading out as we attempted to communicate. From what I could tell, this Brazilian farmer had a small field of rice right near mine, and I asked if I could see his stand of rice. We traveled less than a kilometer to his field, and to my surprise, the his stand of rice wasn't near as tall nor near as close to heading out as mine, even though we planted our fields precisely the same week. He explained he had cleared the patch of land three years prior and planted rice in that field every year since. Each year, the rice field produced less than the year before. I also noticed a golden color on the green stems of the rice. I recognized the disease known as rust from my days in the oat fields of Iowa. Without the benefit of fertilizer in Brazil, the only thing I could tell the farmer was that he had to rotate each planting with some other type of crop to help reduce the chance of disease and total depletion of the soil's nutrients needed for rice. My knowledge ended there for I couldn't think of anything else to help this man. I had no suggestion for what to rotate the crops with. I headed back to Coari pondering the problem for I knew full well I would be facing the very same issue in the near future.

On Monday, November 18, we received our first egg from the pullets. I thought the kids were pulling one on me. When I first saw the egg, I couldn't believe they were laying eggs already. These hens were only four and a half months old, and it turned out to be true because we had gotten eggs every day since. Word spread around town, and nobody could believe it because it usually took the local chickens a whole year to lay their first egg. In comparison, one person living near the chicken project had baby chicks on the ground. When our first chickens arrived, these local chickens weren't even close to a pound while our hybrid chickens were four and five pounds and already laying eggs.

Right after the first egg was laid, Raul, Alphonso, and I built four really cute nesting boxes. While we did this, we watched a young pullet go right over, jump into the first nesting box, and settle in. The boys got so excited they could hardly work, and they kept going over to the pullet and gently moved her to see if she laid something. Needless to say, after several times of doing this, the pullet became nervous and left the box without any results. Every egg that was found since then was in the nesting boxes.

About the same time in mid-November, we started to get reports back that some of the pullets we sold as a couple had started laying eggs. That was when the trouble manifested itself. Alphonso and Raul told me that some of the people who had bought the two chickens as a couple had reservations as to the morality of the couple. The boys related to me that the hybrid chickens kept laying eggs and would not interrupt their laying process to stop and sit on the eggs they had laid to hatch. Allegedly, the hen was a creature of ill repute and considered to be some type of a "whore." That didn't go down well in this community. This rumor had no trouble in spreading because some of the people were already suspicious of these chickens not raised by their mothers. Some of the Brazilians had the attitude that it was okay for the male to have multiple partners, but it was a definite no for the females. After all, the female had to keep her partner happy at home and raise the offspring. The native chickens currently populating the backyards were a breed of fighting chicken, which grew tall and very lean with hardly any meat on their bones. It was in the hen's nature to turn broody right after laying a few eggs and start sitting on the eggs for hatching. At this rate, the hens would only produce about thirty offspring annually. The males were so tough and full of corded muscle that there wasn't much meat on their tall bones.

I had to think fast if I were to head off this latest dilemma. I came up with the idea that, when a couple was sold, the boys and I would talk about how wonderful the hen was and how she wanted many children. In order to do that, she would have to keep laying eggs. To help her do that, the hybrid hen would need one of the skinny old hens to assume the duty of sitting on the eggs, kind of like a "grandmother hen." When the chicks would hatch, the old hen could teach the young pupils how to scratch and eat, and the chicks could live alongside their mothers. In order to get this message across, when the people came to buy the couples, we would have to detain them as long as possible and, at the same time, explain the verbal contract. I knew the Brazilians could buy into the concept of the old cluck being the "grandmother," which wasn't too different from their home life as many layers of extended family were in their own homes. That way, it was explained that the hybrid hen could continue to lay more eggs so there would be more brothers and sisters for the chicks. If too many eggs were laid before the old hen was ready to sit on the nest again, the eggs could be consumed as food for the people in the family. It took some time before the dissatisfaction subsided, but the people who owned the hybrid hen and rooster couple eventually recognized the merits of owning hybrid chickens.

By the time the first batch of chickens were mature, the first chicken house was empty and ready for another batch. Minor repairs had to be completed on the first house because all of the bamboo used as walls was paper thin from the termite infestation. The floor had to be scraped of the entire chicken residue and removed. Some equipment, such as the self-feeding water supply, had rusted through and needed to be replaced. Termites were a constant issue, and the roof rafters of both houses and other parts of the structures had to be periodically inspected. Termites have a very important role in Brazil by being very aggressive on any wood that was not growing, thus helping the jungle to renew itself.

———

Between major building projects, Ed would take on other projects when asked. With the recent Vatican II Council, changes were in the way Mass was offered so the local church needed a smaller altar that could be used for the priest to face the congregation. Along with that change, the Mass was to be in the vernacular, meaning it would be offered in the native tongue where the Mass was being celebrated instead of the usual Latin. Ed agreed to design and build an altar for that purpose. After spending much time designing the altar on paper and gathering the exact kind of wood he needed, Ed started to build the altar in a room next to the fathers' tractor and generator. I always enjoyed being with Ed so I would sit for hours on end talking to Ed while he worked away. Ed spent a lot of time on every part of the altar project because he was such a perfectionist. One day in the final days of sanding the altar, Ed asked me to hand him wood from the rafters above the altar. When I reached for the piece, another large piece of wood came crashing down right in the middle of the altar, putting a huge dent in the altar. I will never forget the look on Ed's face as he inspected the damage. I felt like dying right there as Ed assured me that it was okay and he would be able to get the dent out somehow. I knew in my gut that it wasn't okay and I should have been much more careful. Ed applied a small amount of water on the dented part of the bare wood's surface. With several careful applications of water, the dented wood eventually absorbed it, and the dent swelled up and almost disappeared. Some of the dent never did come out, and I feel guilty yet today for what I did to Ed's beautiful altar.

———

About this same time, a man named Lucindo, an employee of the Brazilian government, arrived by the amphibious airplane and was invited to stay upstairs with Ray, Ed, and me for there was no such thing as a hotel in Coari. Lucindo was to study the quality of education being presented to the children of Coari, including the Redemptorist school and the public school system.

I hoped Lucindo would be able to help resolve what I considered a rather serious issue with the Brazilian postal system. Despite repeated warnings, my mother sent me two pair of blue jeans, several rolls of film, and some T-shirts in a package intended for me. The Brazilian government seized the package and opened it to inspect its contents. They imposed a duty of over $250, over ten times its original value. Even with the intervention of the fathers, the postal system would not budge, and this dispute had been going on for months. In conversation with Lucindo, I mentioned this dispute, and he calmly assured me that he would take care of it when he returned to Manaus.

Lucindo, a very intelligent man, was great to talk to about the attitude of the military government that was currently in power. Lucindo was very patient with my Portuguese. In one conversation with Lucindo, he teased me about girls, and I conveyed I was shy around them, but, in doing so, I used the Portuguese word *galenia* for the American slang of "chicken." The word barely left my lips, and Lucindo shrank back in horror. This was where Lucindo's patience was at its best as he told me the word I had used to describe my shyness was really the slang for "homosexual" and I was never to translate American slang literally into Portuguese. I felt like I was back in Iowa at Calvary Cemetery when Bob and Raul would test different words. I also learned from Lucindo never to use the phrase, "Run like a deer," because that also had a very different meaning in Brazil, much akin to using the word "chicken."

Lucindo told me that one's twenty-fourth birthday was never celebrated in Brazil due to the connotation inferring that the number twenty-four was slang for being gay. Lucindo also suggested that most high-rise buildings would just skip the number twenty-four and go from the twenty-third to the twenty-fifth floor.

During Lucindo's stay, I got to air out several ideas I had developed about Brazil. Lucindo, in turn, was able to clear up many notions Brazilians had about the United States. Lucindo told me that it was okay for a Brazilian to have an American as a friend but still not like Americans as a whole. There was a deep-seated feeling that the United States was considered an economically imperialist nation. The Brazilians believed the United States invested money in Brazil only to extract profits and did very little or cared slightly about raising the living standards of Brazilians. As a whole, Brazil felt their resources were being exploited and they should be the ones benefiting from it. I could tell from Lucindo's tone that he believed this, and I knew it was difficult to argue with.

Lucindo also related to me that it was a difficult concept for most Brazilians to grasp that American priests, sisters, brothers, and Papal Volunteers would give up so much comfort and wealth of the United States for the conditions in Brazil without gaining back something materially.

Lucindo's stay lasted for three weeks. About a month after his departure, my package arrived through the fathers with just a two-dollar charge. A saying was very prevalent in Brazil, "It wasn't what you knew in Brazil that mattered, but it mattered more on who you knew." In this case, it must have been true.

All the above notions were hard to grapple with in the Brazilian mind when they could only think about going to the United States and living like a king. Weather permitting, on a monthly basis, the town's government would arrange for a huge white sheet to be hung between some trees in the plaza to serve as a movie screen. One particular movie that set the whole town buzzing with excitement was *Breakfast at Tiffany's*. In the film, nobody paid cash for anything. And if someone did pay for something, he simply signed a small piece of paper, and off he would go. It was difficult to explain the concept of checks and credit cards to the natives of Coari, especially when none of them used the banking system at all. Films like this only fueled some Brazilians suspicions as to why we were really there in Brazil. So it was easy to see why they would pine for going to the United States, but one question that came up all too often was, "Am I too black to go to America?" To me, that was a very difficult question to just explain away, considering the then attitude toward civil rights in America.

One way to seek out a living was to fish the Amazon. Sometimes when an especially good catch was made, word would spread, and the trophy fish would be on display by the boat. The crew was quick to brag about the fish and its capture. One type of fish highly sought after was called *Peixe boyi*[17] *or cowfish because the flesh of the fish was firm and tasted like beef. It was believed that this species of fish lived solely on the grass that grew on the bottom of the river, and it would reach weights of over one hundred pounds. A lot of grass was growing in the Amazon. Another highly sought after fish was the Tambaci,* which would also grow to nearly a hundred pounds and was able to feed many people. Its white flesh was more like codfish, and it was also very tasty.

On very special occasions such as a wedding, huge river turtles, which were highly prized, would be the main course. To prepare the feast, the turtle meat was removed totally from the shell. When prepared, the meat was placed back into the upside-down shell and served. The turtle feast was one of the most memorable foods I tasted in Brazil, and the Brazilians knew how to prepare it just right.

For little kids in the United State, fishing was a treat and fun, but for the younger set in Brazil, this wasn't the case. For the ones about age six and many others, it was their daily task to fish and help put food on the table. Most of the horror stories about piranha in the waters of the Amazon had been farfetched and embellished as to their ferociousness. Piranhas were very plentiful in all waters of the Amazon, and there were many different species to be caught. Most of the fish these young anglers caught were of some species of piranha. The piranhas performed the same duty in the Amazon water as the vultures did on land. Piranha helped keep the river free of decaying flesh, usually other fish.

Another species that suffers from embellished stories is the boa constrictor. These snakes do grow to huge lengths, and when one is hungry, it kills its prey by wrapping around its victim and crushing it to death by squeezing the victim until it was dead. But the boa constrictor isn't constantly on the prowl. In fact, this snake will stay in seclusion for long periods of time, up to a month. This snake does not stalk humans

---

[17] Pay-she-boy

but rather avoids us at all costs. Another fable that was rather prevalent along the Amazon was that a boa constrictor would solely seek out human children. The snake would reportedly lay in wait for the birth of a child and devour the infant immediately after the birth. Folklore would have it that this usually happened while the mother rested from all the work and stress of labor. To avoid this calamity from happening, someone had to stand guard for a length of time to protect the mother and the baby.

The rabbit project continued to struggle, and the female rabbit was having a hard time with conception. She and the buck had mated several times without any results. To add to the problem, the priest announced from the pulpit one Sunday that the doe would give birth to baby rabbits on November 11 so the whole congregation would ask me what happened. This same father was on hand for the first mating attempt, and since then, he suspected I didn't know what I was doing. It was one of those things that I couldn't fake and pretend I didn't understand the locals' questions.

On November 10, one hundred chicks arrived via airplane, and only six had expired. I had learned that the chicks had been left out all night at the airport in Manaus, and I was sure the exposure didn't do them well. The other three hundred would be coming shortly and in several batches.

I had been getting ribbed during this time on my farming skills because of three episodes. First, the female rabbit had finally conceived, and her due date had to be extended to the very end of the month. Everyone was on my case about where the baby rabbits were. Second, we had separated twenty hens for laying purposes, and we had three roosters among the count. Third, I brought home a rooster for the cook, and when she was butchering it, she came across this egg sack within the "rooster."

By November 17, no more new chicks had arrived because of plane connections.

I mused to myself, "Wait until I tell the one hundred chicks that are already here that the other chickens had missed their connections."

The new chickens were really droopy and acted like they were sleeping standing up. Their crops were really hard. That normally meant that their digestive systems weren't working properly. Raul had failed to put the small chicks back into their cardboard shipping box the night before so all of them could huddle and retain their body heat during the coolest part of the night. I was also going to return to the chicken house and check on the baby chicks before I went to bed, but because it was windy and rainy, I didn't want to be in my canoe in that kind of weather. So I also failed to go. I felt so bad when I thought of how these little chicks were left to themselves to huddle to stay warm. I decided I would chew out Raul, who had failed to do his duty. I felt like locking him in the chicken house all night to fend against the cold and mosquitoes to see what it was like.

Raul came to work late the next day. The most disappointing part was that this lad had been the most eager and trustworthy of the two, and he was such a good person. I was so shocked at his failure.

To help prevent this in the future, we also contracted with a man to make us a self-designed incubator/heater for the chickens at night. My idea was to use a kerosene lantern for heat and build tin walls around it to retain the heat. But it couldn't be finished right away yet I needed it now for those sick chicks. We were already down to ninety-one.

Letter to Home
November 17, 1965

Hello to everyone. It sure has been good of all you to write as often as you have. Your letters are like a tonic to me, and they keep me going. Now to answer your questions about the Brazil nuts. The nuts form inside this almost perfectly round, hard shell that is the size of a softball and is found hanging in the tree about sixty feet from the ground. Normally, fourteen nuts are inside the shell, and the shell of the Brazil nut is also very hard and durable. It is like the Lord overdid the sturdiness factor when he made these. Upon maturity, the shell and nuts weigh about one and a half pounds, and these shells would come hurdling to the ground when ripe. It is safe to say that it is not wise to walk or rest under these Brazil nut trees when these shells come down. The locals gather the shells up and chop them open with large corn knives to gain access to the nuts inside. You cannot crack these shells with a hammer, nor can you break them by smashing them onto a rock or cement, for I have tried. Now you get some idea the power of the beaks of the macaws and the close call I had when I put my finger in one macaw's mouth. Father Zenk, our new director of the Iowa Papal Volunteers in the US, visited the rabbit project and urged me to turn the project entirely over to the boys for this director has other plans for me. I have no idea what he was referring to, but it does seem worth looking into. Sending my love to all, Marvin

Some of the baby chicks that had arrived were sick, and about twenty had died so far. We culled out the really sick ones, and I took them back to the Papal Volunteers' house. On the way, I could only imagine what Margaret's reaction to their arrival would be. To my surprise, she jumped right in and tried a few remedies herself. When I told Margaret that I thought their problem was a muscular issue, Margaret and Aparacedia fed the chicks some rice grains that were boiled in salty water. Margaret told me that, when people come to the hospital with muscular weakness, they put them on a high saline diet. While she was explaining, one of the chicks stood up, hopped out of the box, and started peeping. We continued to monitor the treatment, and it seemed to work. The chicks left back at the chicken house continued to do okay, and some of them started growing their wing feathers already.

The rabbit project continued to be a problem. The female doe rabbit had missed her due date to give birth, and I was beginning to suspect the male rabbit was shooting blanks. I heard another guy in town had rabbits so I decided to consult with him. It would be good to introduce an outside bloodline as well because I learned the couple we were trying to mate with each other was possibly brother and sister.

While waiting for the rice to mature, I tried to locate some sort of a combine or device to harvest the rice, but to no avail. It soon became apparent that we would have to harvest the rice by hand. Each trip out to the rice field confirmed the harvest was getting fairly close. I also observed that the dreaded disease of rust was starting to appear in my field as well, and the disturbing thing was that I could tell exactly where someone had entered the field and where he walked for the rust disease also appeared there. I was sure the same farmer I had visited earlier had made several trips back into my field since. The main point of entry into the field was most convenient, and everyone who entered there carried the rust fungus wherever he went. Obviously, the rust fungus and the maturity of the rice were in a dead heat to the finish. It was often difficult to get out to the field because of mud or scheduling, but the locals were more than willing to keep me informed. Several of the locals, who claimed to know about rice, said I shouldn't have planted the rice in a broadcast manner like oats or wheat back home but should have planted it in small clumps. I wasn't so sure, and only time would tell. I did know that it had been drier than normal, and I was sure the clump-style planting would have suffered from the lack of ample rains as well. When I asked what the logic in planting in clumps was, the local "experts" would give various reasons, but the most common included that it was much easier to plant, there wasn't a need to till the whole area, and it was easier to harvest because the crop was in concentrated spots. I hadn't heard anything about planting in clumps that would increase the yield of rice. I knew the locals had no power equipment to rely on so I did understand their logic of planting in clumps, but I knew the three acres would produce tenfold of the clump process.

Padre Jamie arranged for ten workers, and I started the process of stripping the rice seed from the stalks and placing the seed into burlap sacks, all the while cognizant of the fire ants and spiders living in the soil. By the time we handpicked the entire field, we had harvested forty bags of rice. Each bag weighed fifty kilograms, or a total of two tons. When we hauled the rice back to Coari on the town's truck, we found no source to mill the rice because all the rice in Coari had been shipped in. No mills were in Coari. The solution was to load the rice directly onto a boat that would take the rice downriver to the nearest mill. Rather than have the rice hauled back to Coari, the rice was sold to the miller, and the proceeds were intended for the chicken project. The needed funds came just in time for future investment. There was, however, a lot of talk around town on how much rice had been harvested, and everyone marveled at the yield.

On December 14, 1965, my vacation started a day earlier than anticipated because one of the fathers came to me to ask a favor. He had officiated at a wedding, and the groom told him a hard luck story. The new couple couldn't get on the airplane the next day to go on their honeymoon because the plane tickets were all sold out and the bride couldn't get a ticket. The father knew about my vacation plans and asked me to give up my plane ticket for the next day. The fathers' boat was leaving in an hour, and he was sure I could make it. Not wanting to spoil a honeymoon and knowing I owed a few favors to the fathers anyway, I agreed. Down here, one must be ready to grant a favor if one were to receive a favor.

I traveled downriver by the fathers' boat instead, and the trip took two days downriver, but it was a good, relaxing start of vacation.

To the surprise of my life, when I got to Manaus, Tony and Dave were unable to take on a traveling guest because Bill, a Papal Volunteer from Iowa, was briefly stationed in Manaus so I had to go to a hotel. The one I wanted would have cost a week's worth of vacation funds per day, and I knew I would be in Manaus for a week. So I rented a room in this dingy ol' rat hole of a hotel while I shopped for supplies and medicines for the chickens. I also contacted a veterinarian just in case I would need one again. I bought some vitamins to add to the chicken's water. I was also able to establish a much-improved source of chicken feed, resulting in more direct handling and faster shipping. Also, the feed would be ground and blended as orders were placed rather than weeks in advance. This would go a long way in reducing the mold factor. I mainly wanted to find out where my order of chickens stood for I had ordered four hundred chickens a long time ago and only received one hundred so far.

One night, I returned to my hotel room, turned the key to the door, and walked in. By the vanity in the room sat this beautiful young lady clad only in a bath towel, combing out her wet hair. I shrank back in horror as I stepped back into the hall to double-check my room number. Sure enough, I was in the right room. I cautiously returned into the room and inquired in my shaken Portuguese as to what she was doing there. She calmly answered that she had just taken a bath and she was combing her hair out. She hoped I wouldn't mind if she stayed a while. I mustered up enough Portuguese to tell her to get out of my room, which she calmly obeyed. I first locked the door again and put a chair under the doorknob. I then proceeded to see if anything was missing from my luggage, and everything was there. From then on, I was much more cautious when entering my room, and I made sure to leave nothing valuable in my suitcase.

Inflation continued to be a problem in Brazil. For example, the airline ticket I priced the day before I bought it went up a good 30 percent on the day I actually purchased it. This seemed to be the standard rate jump when inflation took its grip. I had vowed to myself that I would never beg for additional money from home, but it was getting to be a very dire situation, especially when traveling.

While in Manaus, I had a very good time visiting with other Papal Volunteers from Iowa: Mary Jo, Lucille, and Kitty. Mary Jo was the sweetest person. She was rather slight in stature, but that appearance was deceiving if one thought she was too frail to handle Brazil. Lucille could put everything into perspective. Kitty would listen to our conversations. Just at the right time, she would blink her eyes as she would inject her wisdom. Kitty was of few words, but when she spoke, everyone would listen. The female Papal Volunteers had the largest residence and the most space to host get-togethers, and it was a delight to meet and converse with them as I made my way to Belem.

Letter to Home
December 24, 1965

Hello, everyone. Christmastime is supposed to be a time of joy and happiness, but I sure do get homesick because of all the time I am away from home. I have many close friends with the Volunteers, but I really miss all of you. I realize the tape recording I sent home was not too chipper, especially with the time of the year it is. I thought being away from home the first Christmas was really hard, but this one seems much more difficult, and you don't know how close you came to having an extra mouth to feed for Christmas dinner. It isn't just the season that is depressing, but I feel that everything is unraveling for the Papal Volunteers. Consumer prices are out of sight, several close Volunteers have returned to the US before their time was up, and there are rumors of trouble in paradise with the fathers and the Volunteers in Coari, which is the first I have heard. I may have to transfer and leave all of my projects and then relocate somewhere else and start all over. On December 30, I fly back to visit the farm in Santarem. From there, I will travel back upriver by airplane to Manaus and join Ray, who will be going back to Coari as well. I look forward to this traveling together for I hate to travel alone. Please do not let my feeling of homesickness dampen your Christmastime for I know this is just the weight of the season. I have been praying a lot, and I know God is with me. I keep reminding myself that God will never expect more of me then what I am capable of. The best thing you can do is keep those wonderful letters of support and love coming my way and I will be okay. May the love of the Christ Child be with all of you this Christmas season. Love, Marvin

---

Being in Belem over Christmas was a very gratifying time for me, and I made the most of it by going to all the Christmas parties and dining out with some other Papal Volunteers stationed near and around Belem. I got to know Dave and Savena, another married couple from Kansas. Dave's projects were teaching construction methods, and Savena was a nurse who worked at Guadalupe Hospital.

I also got to know two other Papal Volunteers, John and Frannie, a married couple from Kansas. I had met John before while I was studying in Casa Central. While there, Frannie gave birth to their first child, and everyone marveled at the blond baby boy. Frannie's project was working as a nurse at Guadalupe Hospital, and John served as procurator for the hospital. While I was there, I connected with Brother Norbert in Santarem. I advised him that I was going to stop by the farm and see him for I had a lot of questions about farming in Brazil.

Letter to Home
January 2, 1966

Hello to everyone. Here I am in Santarem once again, and I will be here a week before heading back to Coari. I plan to get to Coari on January 12. I think most things are settled now, and I know I feel much better after that brief respite. Sorry about the down-in-the-mouth attitude through Christmas. This vacation has really helped me get my feet back on the ground, and I am so fortunate to be able to visit with a lot of other Papal Volunteers. Their support has made me realize that I am not in this alone. Another big boost in my morale will be all the letters awaiting me when I get back to Coari. Thanks again for all of your love and understating. Love, Marvin

---

When I landed in Santarem, I first arranged for a trip out to the farm where Brother Norbert was. The odd thing was being in the Amazon jungle and yet seeing the effects of a major drought. Everything was dying on the land that had been cleared for future crops. It hadn't rained in over a month, and the last rain was so little that it didn't help relieve the situation. The untouched part of the jungle seemed to be handling the drought quite well, however. What crops that could have been planted had been held back for the last three months due to the lack of rain. The local farmers in and around Santarem highly respected Brother Norbert for none of them would make a move in their fields until he did. The last drought here was in 1958, and every crop failed. The people suffered very much for everyone depended so much on the land and its produce. Brother Norbert, being a typical farmer, was an eternal optimist, and he predicted ample rain would start soon.

On the way back to Coari, I was glad to stay in Manaus for three days. Kitty, in her wonderful wisdom, helped me to be not so apprehensive of the future and all the changes that were coming down.

Her short message hit home when, with her eyes blinking, she wisely said, "Is it not you who are affecting change in Coari? Then why would you be so afraid of another change?"

I had time to think about that on my way back upriver.

Letter to Home
January 23, 1966

Hello Mom, Dad, and everyone. What a vacation I had, and the best part was staying in Santarem. I am back in Coari now, and I was expected back about a week ago, but here is what happened. When I flew into Manaus, I started looking right away for a fare to Coari, and I was willing to go by boat, plane, or whatever, but nothing was to be found. The hotel I was staying at was more expensive than the first one I stayed at, but I wanted to avoid the first one that I had a bad experience with. To my surprise, two priests I studied with in Belem are now based in Manaus, and they graciously invited me to stay with them. I lunged at the chance for I had no idea how long it would take to get a plane ticket. Just after settling in, I was lucky enough to be at the plane ticket counter when I was able to snap up a ticket that someone else had just cancelled, so I was on a roll of good breaks. That is until I was at the Redemptorist house in Manaus and I met Padre Marcus, our boss in Coari, and his mother who was visiting from the US. Once Padre Marcus learned I had just procured a plane ticket to Coari, his face lit up, and he informed me that they also had a ticket to fly that particular day. I should have paid more attention to the word "a" ticket when the two of them were together. To make a long story short, Padre Marcus again asked for a favor by asking me to give my ticket to his mother so she could fly as well. He added that the fathers' boat would have room for me when it left in three days or so. What else could I do but cave in for I was no longer paying for the hotel and the boat trip would be free? So with the three-day delay and the three days journeying upriver, I arrived back a week late. So that is the second time I gave up my plane tickets to go on a boat cruise instead. I hope and trust all is well there, and please do keep the letters flowing. I love you all, and I cannot wait to get home. Love, Marvin

---

Upon my return to Coari, I saw the chickens were doing great, and we were getting about a dozen eggs a day. One particular day, we got seventeen eggs out of nineteen hens. Raul and Alphonso recounted to me how they were working in the chicken house that day and they said the hens were all lined up waiting for the nesting boxes. The second orders of chickens were finally all here, but it took three different deliveries to get to the 375 that now resided in the first chicken house. Because of the three different deliveries, we had three different sizes of chickens to deal with, and we were nearing the end of our feed again. Someone failed to order more feed while I was gone, and I could only pray the feed would make it before we ran out. We had experienced only a few cases of chicken pox in one of the batches, which we treated right away. The hybrid hen eggs were being sold out every day, and we were charging the equivalent of six cents per egg. As we sold them, we cautioned the buyers not to purchase them for eating but rather to hatch with their own brood, using the old clucks in their backyards. Raul and Alphonso both related that they knew of quite a few people who had purchased the hybrid eggs. They personally saw several old clucks and their brood of hybrid chicks scratching in the dirt in several backyards. When I asked Raul and Alphonso if these people feared the chickens would be stolen, they related on how locals dealt with thieves.

Raul, with his big brown eyes bugging out of his head, said, "When a thief is caught, his hand is immediately chopped off with a machete."

With huge eyes, Alphonso slowly nodded in agreement. I believed them for they appeared very serious, and there was no hint of trickery this time.

I then said, "The process must work for I haven't seen any one-handed people around."

Alphonso responded, "When it does happen, that person just disappears into the jungle for the locals won't permit him to live in the community. If he tried to go somewhere else to another community, he would be run off."

With the addition of four hundred more chickens, more feeders were necessary, and everyone was amazed at how we devised a self-water system for the hens. We constructed the system in the very same way as before. We would fill the can with the aid of a plastic hose and a funnel, and when the can was full, we would turn it over. Using this method, the chickens would have water all day, and we didn't have to keep filling pans or trays. We were able to keep feed and water in front of over four hundred head of chickens.

The very next day, we sold some of the roosters and hens as a married couple from the second batch of chickens, despite the fact the couples were a bit small, but we needed to ration the feed. The locals responded really quickly when word got out that we were having a "fire sale" to sell some of the chickens. We had to find a way to reduce feed consumption until the next batch arrived. The acute lack of food put us back to spending almost all day getting feed for those hungry chickens. Same as before, we purchased shelled corn locally, which we would pound the kernels of corn to break it up. We used the same process for rice kernels. We would then blend the two grains together, along with some powdered milk and cornmeal from the Caritas program. This process had to be continued until a new batch of feed came in by boat.

February brought another cold spell of weather. At night, it got down to sixty or sixty-five degrees. Some of the people would huddle around fifty-five-gallon drums in the middle of the street that were kept burning all night with whatever would burn. The sun would help during the day, but these people would sure suffer at nighttime. This cold season lasted a week or so, and despite the short duration of the cold, many people would come down with illnesses related to exposure. The locals were so original with naming things that they called this time *freasgen*.[18]

The rabbit project was struggling, and while I was on vacation, John seized the chance to have eight female rabbits and three male rabbits delivered. The fathers helped by instructing their resident carpenter to aid in the construction of more rabbit hutches. John and I planned the following. We would bestow a female rabbit to a select family that could use the help and would be trustworthy to care for the rabbits. The rabbits were to be

---

[18] The freezing

three months old, and these families were to care for the doe rabbits for another four months, about the time it took a doe to reach maturity. This would also give the family time to adapt to caring for the rabbits, and it would give time for the rabbits to become familiar with the family, which was a very important step. When the doe reached maturity, the family would bring its doe back to us for breeding. After the first litter of rabbits was born and mature enough, we were to receive a female baby rabbit as payment. The family would get to keep the original doe and future rabbits. The whole idea was to get people to raise their own food, and they could butcher a rabbit without need of refrigeration. This was the same concept that we used with the chickens. John took the opportunity to draw up a written contract in Portuguese to stress the validity of the process.

The original pair of rabbits had given birth to some small litters several times, but each time, the doe rabbit must have become frightened and killed her own young. I really had to stress to the two girls on the rabbit project that they had to make sure they limited the viewing of the baby rabbits to a bare minimum and not to allow anyone else to peek. To prevent this practice, I installed some of the padlocks the nuns had given me in Belem.

The night before Good Friday was April 8, 1966. I decided to spend the whole night in the chicken houses because of a rumored custom that called for some people to prowl the night and steal something, like a chicken they would cook for Holy Saturday, and then have the gall to invite you over to eat it. This was the only time stealing was permitted, and there was no way I was going to let that happen. I spent the night nearly freezing to death, and the mosquitoes attacked me all night. To top that off, no one came, and I had a very sore throat and a good start on a cold. I didn't know if I should have been disappointed or elated for all of my efforts.

On Good Friday, the town of Coari had a huge procession with the living rosary and the Stations of the Cross all mixed into one huge parade. This procession lasted about three hours and stretched across town for more than a mile. I grabbed my camera and took several pictures. One of the most moving was the scene of the Sixth Station, where Veronica wiped the face of Jesus. I was able to get fairly close to the veil as the people acted it out. The crowd was huge, and I was sure everyone in Coari was in attendance. I was able to move about freely without people asking me to take their picture for everyone seemed to be involved in the parade process and its message.

—·····—

The plane that landed on the water was getting quite old. This style of plane was from World War II, and these airplanes were breaking down more and more and for longer periods of time as parts were very scarce. Sources told me that the company that operated this line to Coari only signed a one-year contract, and this contract would be up in a few more short months. The long-range plan included clearing a landing field where my rice was currently growing, so I knew the rice project was short-lived. But I also knew, if the plans to build the airport were to be announced the next day, I would still get several crops in because "this was Brazil."

—·····—

About that time, the Papal Volunteers in Coari received a pleasant surprise from Sioux City. The Chancery Office sent us a film developing kit, and it sure was a lot of fun. Ray and I started immediately developing ten rolls of black-and-white film. We borrowed an enlarger from a guy downtown so we were having a blast. As the lights would go out at nine every night when the generator would shut down, making a darkroom wasn't a problem, and we didn't have to worry about someone turning on the lights by mistake. The light from the streetlights outside was no longer a problem as well. We set up our darkroom in the bathroom because it had running water and plenty of places to hang the filmstrips while they dried. When we ran low on a chemicals, which wasn't very long, we had to wait for someone who was going downriver to buy us more.

I finally received a letter from Brother Norbert, and he said the rains had returned and his field corn was over knee high already despite the late planting. He thanked me for the four hybrid chickens I sent him. I was able to do this when I had heard a family from Coari was traveling to Santarem by passenger boat, and they agreed to look after the young chickens and deliver my makeshift crate to Brother Norbert. I was very glad to hear that the chickens arrived, and I felt very proud to have spread my work around.

Letter to Home
May 18, 1966

Hello to everyone at home. Well, I just got back from a trip to Manaus by flying the Catalina plane that landed on the water. The old girl is getting pretty old, and I sometimes wonder how it keeps going. My seat was close to the water, and when the plane touched down, I got wet from fine spray of water that made its way into the cabin via some fine cracks in the fuselage. Cracks in the fuselage are not uncommon. In fact during this flight, we hit a rainstorm, and the roof started leaking. Out came the handkerchiefs from the passengers to mop up the water. My reason for going to Manaus was to see what the holdup on the feed for the chickens was. To my disappointment, I learned the keeper of the purse strings, namely the Redemptorist Fathers, hadn't authorized the purchase. The reason wasn't a shortage of feed, as I was told. Sometimes, it is very frustrating to have to struggle with the very people you are working with and for. At times like this, I get really disillusioned when I think how the charitable dollars sent down here for charitable projects are being spent. Maybe I am being naïve, but I feel my project will have a much more lasting effect than some of the other causes. It seems to me that the powers-that-be do not realize there is an investment in the future and all the money they allocated so far is tied up in investment. I let a few people know this before I headed back to Coari. It may be at least another week before the next supply boat comes in, so I won't be lacking in something to do until it does. Father Clemente, my boss in Belem, wrote me that the project in Belem isn't ready for me yet, so I won't be transferred for a while. In Brazilian speak, it might be months, or perhaps the project hasn't even been approved or started yet. I'll let you know as this unfolds. Other than that, all is well here, and I trust the same is there. I am enclosing all my love. Love, Marvin

About the end of May, a Brazilian navy boat known as a Corvette came into Coari Lake with some building materials for the fathers. The captain of the huge vessel came in too close, hit a hidden sandbar, and got hung up. The boat itself must have been at least 250 feet long, and I wouldn't even hazard a guess as to its weight. To get it off the sandbar, several smaller boats came out and unloaded the cargo on the Corvette that was intended for Coari. This alone wasn't enough to help get it backed off the sandbar, even after the Corvette raced its powerful engines in full speed in reverse. Many more boats were summoned, and with all of them tugging, they still couldn't move it. Finally after several attempts, which took all day, the Corvette dropped its two-ton anchor off the rear of the ship, and with repeated actions, they were able to winch the ship off the sandbar. A huge crowd had gathered to watch the whole process, and it was the general consensus that the captain of the vessel didn't know what he was doing. Apparently, everyone was right because a huge oil barge from Peru hit the Corvette in the Port of Coari four hours after it left the sandbar. According to some of the many rumors, the Corvette was sailing out of port and around a bend and didn't see the oil barge loaded with oil, and they collided. Both boats were about forty feet offshore, and the barge, traveling at about twelve miles per hour, couldn't stop. The Corvette reportedly turned broadside to try to get out of the way, and the barge hit the Corvette just off the front two compartments, right below the waterline. The Corvette sunk. That part of the rumor turned out to be false because the Corvette didn't sink due to the fast actions of the crew who sealed off the two compartments before it could take on more water. Unfortunately, two navy men died, and only one body was recovered. The other sailor's body couldn't be found and apparently went into the river. This fact halted all forms of fishing around that area for at least a week. None of the locals wanted to take a chance and consume a fish that might had consumed human flesh. The recovered body of the other sailor was flown to Belem for a grand funeral. The accident happened right near the mouth of rivers opening right outside of Coari, and we got a glimpse of the listing naval vessel as it limped away.

Many rumors swirled around the incident, and even though there couldn't have been very many witnesses, those who were spreading the reports were a witness to the mishap. Almost everyone swore it was the country of Peru's fault and the Peruvian government would have to pay big time. I knew at the time that the Brazilian government should act prudently. Peru wasn't too wild about the oil arrangement as it was because, in the trade agreement, coffee was to be traded for oil. The people of Peru felt this arrangement was a big factor in depressing Peru's coffee prices and marketability

It was quite a sight to see these oil barges going up and downriver, which I witnessed on several occasions while sailing the Amazon. When these barges would go upriver empty, the barges would float on top of the water and stand about forty feet above the river's surface while a very powerful tugboat pushed it. I could hear them coming for miles away because they were constantly banging and crashing into each other. Being empty, they made a huge booming sound. Conversely, when these barges were fully loaded and being pushed downriver, the barges were nearly impossible to see because the containers were completely level with the water's surface. One could only see the light post that stuck out of the water four or five feet above the barges themselves, and the barges didn't crash into each other while fully loaded with oil. The only sound to be heard would be the hum of the very powerful engine of the tugboat pushing the barges. So much tonnage was in motion that it would take a long time and a lot of distance to stop, perhaps a mile or so, especially when four or five containers were hooked together.

During that same time, the school in Coari hosted the "Crowning of the Queen of Spring," and I decided to go. The judging of the queen was clearly embarrassingly rigged. The girl who won the beauty contest was ugly as on old mud fence, and she had no theatrical pose whatever. However, this dumpy little girl was the daughter of the wealthiest man in town. It was clear to me and many others that a lot more talent was on the stage that night and the best ones weren't even considered. And to top it off, her sister won the same title last year. Many people were relieved because this girl was the last one in that family. Maybe it would be a fairer contest by next year. After the mud hen was crowned, there was a really fun dance, and I learned a new dance called the bolero, the first Latin dance I ever danced. Several of the young Brazilian girls lined up to dance with the blue-eyed American.

On June 8-10, 1966, all the Papal Volunteers from Manaus and Coari converged on the retreat house of the Redemptorist Fathers, a place called *Pedreas.*[19] Father Steichen, who was from Kansas, had replaced Father Lies as head of the Papal Volunteer program in Kansas. Father Steichen made

---

[19]   Rocky area

the journey all the way down to Brazil to meet the Kansas Papal Volunteers and conduct the retreat for all of us in the Amazon Valley. Offering the Mass in the vernacular was permitted in Brazil, even though it still wasn't allowed in the United States. Father Steichen offered the Mass in English, and all the Papal Volunteers played a major role in the offering, which was quite moving. It was wonderful to be able to see everyone together again as we all must have felt it renewed our mission in Brazil.

When I returned to Coari, I once again got involved in my projects. The rabbit project seemed to be going a little better. The first rabbit pair sent to the interior gave birth to four rabbits, but they all died. According to our instructions, the person who received the rabbits was to bring the doe rabbit right back if this were to happen, which he did. After rebreeding, the doe had been sent back into the interior and was due to give birth around the last day of July. The people here in Coari were just aching to be able to buy little rabbits to care for their own, and I wished we could fulfill their wishes, but it was going to take a little longer. At this point, John was entirely in charge of the rabbit project, along with Lucia and Francesca. John worked continuously to keep the project going, and through his contacts, he was able to get several more pairs of rabbits to be donated to the projects. But in reality, John, Lucia, and Francesca were battling heavy odds on several fronts, which included the oppressive heat, lack of proper hutches in the interior, nutritious food to balance the rabbit's diet, as well as the desire of the Brazilians to constantly handle the rabbits. When a doe was pregnant, the less activity and handling, the better it was for her. If she were frightened in any way, the doe would instinctively destroy her own young at the slightest provocation.

The last I heard, John had twenty-three rabbits out on loan, and several families were able to have them reproduce successfully.

———————

Raul and Alphonso would gather the eggs daily and take them into town to fill orders that were placed days before. I urged the two boys to try to convince the locals to use the eggs for hatching and not just eating. Almost every yard had an old fighting hen that was always willing and able to sit on and incubate the eggs until hatched. We sold several eggs, and I was sure that not all were used for hatching, but it wasn't too long before we started to see hybrid chickens in almost every backyard. Selling the eggs worked especially well because we could sell more eggs to those who couldn't afford a pair of chickens as a couple and we could maintain the health of the flock. Sometimes, it was difficult to convince those who owned the hybrids to supplement the nutritional level of food and to convince them that just scratching around on the ground would not sustain the chicken's health. I could sense the growing uneasiness of both boys on the project, and I repeatedly had to stress that the money being collected had to be reinvested in more chickens and more housing for the chickens. There simply wasn't enough money to support a decent living salary for both boys and to continue the project as it stood. The boys weren't totally convinced of this and often commented on all the money that was coming in by selling eggs and hen and rooster couples.

Padre Jamie was an excellent assistant to Padre Marcus, and he had his hand in many things. Besides helping me with my projects, Padre Jamie managed to coordinate projects up and down the Amazon. It was nothing to learn that Padre Jamie was the catalyst behind many programs, including the construction of chapels and meeting centers along the Amazon. Padre Jamie got behind the completion of the bridge across the lagoon that separated Coari from the area called Chagas, where my chicken houses stood and where I traveled every day by canoe. Several politicians got into office by promising the population of approximately one thousand people on the Chagas side to complete the bridge. After doing a little construction, it stopped once they took office. The area was a backwater steam that filled up and divided the city while the Amazon was at its crest for eight months of the year. As a result, Chagas had no market, church, schools, or access to a medical facility. Water taxis (makeshift canoes) transported the children over to schools. On many occasions, the canoes would swamp, and the children would have to swim to shore. Only a few deaths occurred over the years, but countless shoes and books were lost. Having enough of this, Padre Jamie contacted the Brazilian government and, with an engineer's help, worked out a plan. A cement bridge was out of the question due to its expense, but Padre Jamie contacted Chico Correa, who had only eight years of school but proved himself by establishing an industrial park in Coari and running his own business.

The rich gave money at fund-raisers, workers agreed to work at a cut rate, and only the bricklayers refused to yield to a lower rate. The most primitive means hewn and carried logs over forty-five feet long out of the jungle. The wood chosen was very dense and heavy, so it wouldn't float. Many workers often had to drag it. Women and children carried bricks to the project. Everyone from both sides of the water got involved. Then the water came back into the lagoon, and all work ceased. Eight months later, the water again receded, but by that time, everyone lost interest. Chico began his campaign again, but the response was minimal. Padre Jamie helped with his voice, but several other projects bogged him down.

The mayor of the city said, "Forget it."

Chico didn't give up and used his own money to hire a few workers. On October 21, 1965, he was able to get the first column, weighing over four tons, up. But trouble still plagued Chico, such as no funds, solid footing in the soil, or bricks for the footing. But somehow, before the water returned, twenty-eight pillars were erected, all on solid brick footings. Everyone who knew Chico wasn't surprised, and they knew that, when the water would go down next year, Chico would be back at it.

During the high water period of eight months, the mayor of the city saw the political value down the road and threw his weight behind the project. When the water receded, the rest of the bridge was assembled by cutting notches in the wood and then binding the pieces by strong ropes. Not a single nail was used in the whole construction. At the grand opening, the whole town came to admire and give homage to their own, Crazy Chico, as everyone liked to call him. The bridge transformed that side of town called Chagas. In time, Chagas was no longer considered the wrong side of town to live in.

A very large school was near completion in Coari, and the Redemptorist Fathers would operate it as a regional seminary. Plans included turning the chicken project over to the seminary as soon as the school was staffed and filled with students. I was to be still in charge but at a different level. I lost the two boys, as Raul answered his call to the seminary for the priesthood and Alphonso focused his attention on the pursuit of girls and no longer wanted to be part of the chicken project. Looking back, the two boys saw a lot of money, especially for them, being exchanged. They both understood that some of the money had to be reinvested, but not all of it. Alphonso especially was always after me about money, and he wanted to take some of the profits and spend it on his other pursuits. I kept telling them that there would be a time when that would be possible, but not before the project got large enough. I projected to them that one more additional building had to be built, and we would have to turn at least one thousand chickens a year. Once we achieved that, there would be a fairly good salary for both of the boys. I explained to them that we could achieve this in six more months, which seemed a very short time to me, but to the boys, that was a lifetime.

———

I knew my time was growing short in Coari, and I would enjoy taking my camera and canoe and paddling around in the lagoon, just spending time taking photos and thinking. Several times while I was out there, I missed some great shots of huge fish jumping out of the water. I guessed that some of these fish would exceed one hundred pounds. I would often try to photograph this immense school of small fish swimming very close to the surface. The size of the school would cover over an acre. Every now and then, right in the center of the school, a very large patch of fish would jump out of the water in unison, and a larger fish would break the surface in pursuit of the smaller fish. One photo I prize yet today was of a young man standing on the very front of his canoe, casting a huge net into the lagoon and hoping to snag small fish. This photo is on the cover of this book. It was a fascinating time for me, and I would invariably hate to paddle back in and face all the trials and feelings of uncertainty.

———

On July 28, I made a trip downriver via a public transportation line of boats to gather supplies and order another batch of chickens. The chicken and rabbit projects were still experiencing food supply problems, and at times, there was a bottleneck of funding. The fathers seemed to be still not totally convinced that the project would soon be theirs. Even though every *cruzerio* was being turned over to them, they seemed to fail to realize that the income coming in was much greater than the financial needs. Also, the fathers failed to realize the potential of this project in the future. Not unlike the two boys, most of the money the fathers saw going into the project was in the setup. Major profits were in the future and yet to come.

Traveling on the public riverboat, I took the usual precautions by staying away from the water that was served at meals, but despite my safeguards, I ingested something that created a wild turbulence in my stomach. I could hear all sorts of noises, day and night, that were coming from my stomach and lower intestines. It sounded as if the Indy 500 were going full throttle, and my lower intestines eventually got involved as well. I usually looked forward to these trips on the river, but the trip was a real trial this time, and I felt I was getting more ill each day. On the trip back, I was lucky enough to get a ride the fathers' boat, thus making the competition for the bathroom down to just a few people. No matter what I ate or drank, I had to be on the toilet within a minute or less, only to experience untold thunderous gas and blasting of the porcelain. If I failed to reach the bathroom in time, I would be facing a serious cleanup process.

I hoped that, once I got back to Coari, Margaret would reach into her bag of tricks and administer the cure. Margaret did her best and dispensed the strongest of her medications. Some of these medications did help for a time by reducing the severe bouts of diarrhea and thunderous evacuations of the lower bowel. In a short time, however, these painful bouts would reoccur. Margaret advised me to head downriver to Belem for professional treatment. I was losing weight from my already small frame, and I didn't have any weight to spare. Whenever I set foot outside in my weakened state, many people expressed concern for my appearance.

Several people were very blunt in their appraisal of my health. "Mario, you are going to die!"

Padre Marcus agreed with Margaret's opinion, and he arranged for me to go downriver. With his influence, he arranged a room for me on the commercial Snappe cruise line, a large public ship line that carried passengers and freight up and down the Amazon.

The word had come as well that my new position was ready in Belem. I wasn't to worry for the brothers' school would take over all of my projects immediately. Once I took the cure for the happening in my stomach, I was to stay in Belem and work there. The next morning, I boarded the big ship, and I was grateful to find my space right beside the bathrooms. As the huge ship pulled out of Coari, I stood on the top deck, and it suddenly hit me.

"This is happening so quickly, and I'm not coming back. This is it for Coari."

Tears welled up in my eyes as I recalled Dr. Johnson's words, "You won't cry when you leave home, but you will cry when you leave Brazil."

He was right. There I was, bawling like a baby. It wasn't just my stomach that was churning.

It was a very brief stopover at Manaus because my condition was worsening. I was starting to pass blood and not small amounts either. As soon as possible, I boarded an airplane flight to Belem with the destination of Guadalupe Hospital in mind. When I was weighed at the hospital, I was down to ninety pounds and still losing weight. While getting dressed once, I pulled on my slacks and reached for a belt. Before I knew it, my slacks laid on the floor around my feet. I had lost so much weight that there was nothing to hold up my pants. My whole hind end was gone, and my belt had no more notches

When I got to Guadalupe Hospital, Dr. Martinis took me on as his patient and started my treatment immediately. When I went to the bathroom that first day, the medicine made my urine very dark brown. The next day, it was very blue in color. On the third day, my urine was orange. I continued to lose weight, and I was having extreme pains in my kidneys and stomach. I felt like I was going to exceed the predictions of the people in Coari when they predicted my demise. Despite the IVs, I was still losing fluids faster than the body could absorb. Then a second IV was placed in my other arm as I expressed my desire to go home to the United States and enter a hospital near my parents in Iowa. To my surprise, my wish was granted. After three days in Guadalupe Hospital, I was on a flight bound for the United States. On the long flight back, I had time to think about all the time spent in Brazil, and this thought occurred to me.

I went to Brazil with the intent of setting the world on fire, but Brazil would just not burn. It must have been too green!

CHAPTER 8

HEADING HOME TO IOWA

I don't remember much about the flight from Belem to the United States for I was too ill and weak. Everything I did required an immense effort to keep from having an accident in my underwear. I knew that, if I would consume even the smallest of food or liquid, I would have to be in the bathroom within seconds. That wasn't always possible on the plane. I wasted no time in Miami after getting through customs. I deposited all the mail and packages sent back with me into the first United States postal box I saw, remembering all the favors done for me. During the short time there, I couldn't believe the fast pace. Everybody was in a hurry, and the fascinating thing was that I could understand everything being said, even though I was seldom spoken to directly. I immediately boarded a flight bound for Kansas City. Once there, I hopped a smaller plane bound for Sioux Falls, South Dakota, where I knew my parents would be waiting. I paid no attention to the flight schedule of that small plane.

When the airplane first touched down, I looked out the window and saw familiar sights. Before the plane had stopped rolling to a stop, I was up and pushed my way to the front of the line. I hurriedly disembarked and hastened to the terminal. My first stop was the bathroom. The bowels were starting to settle down, and I was confident that I would soon be in my parents' arms. As I made my way back to the disembarking point, there were no familiar faces.

Maybe my family is late and they'd soon be here.

Twenty minutes went by. I approached the boarding gate and asked if the plane had arrived early. The person at the counter said the plane was right on schedule and would soon be leaving for Sioux Falls.

Horrified, I asked, "Isn't this Sioux Falls?"

The ticket agent said, "No, this Sioux City, Iowa."

No wonder I recognized the surroundings. I had been to the airport several times when I took John to the airport when he flew back to Milwaukee. I panicked as the ticket agent grabbed my ticket and agreed I should be in Sioux Falls. Quickly, the man ran out on to the runway and attempted to flag down the plane speeding down the runway. To no avail, the plane lifted off and was gone. When the agent got back to the desk, he advised me that I could catch another plane to Sioux Falls in another hour. I poured out my sad story to him. He advised me not to panic. He would phone the terminal in Sioux Falls that I would be on the next incoming flight.

I spent the hour near the closest bathroom, and I've never had an hour go by so slowly in my life as I waited for the next flight. Finally on board, I flew the short ninety miles to Sioux Falls. I will never forget the look on my mother's face when her gaze met mine. Immediately, she broke down and cried a lot. I could tell she feared for my health, and my dad just stared at my emaciated frame. My oldest brother, Jerry, was very upset because my two-year-old niece was beside herself from waiting so long. They had been waiting for close to two hours for my arrival. Greetings between all of us were brief as Jerry herded all of us to the car.

Everyone was very anxious for me to tell my story of being in Brazil, but the words wouldn't come out. I had no idea where to start, nor did I know it would be so hard to relate. With every thought that came to me, I felt I would have to explain everything for it was all so different in the United States. I first noticed that everything was so loud and fast-paced. Everyone seemed to be in such a hurry, and every media was loudly hawking something to sell or buy. I immediately yearned for the slower pace of Brazil, and I couldn't figure out if the American people ever slowed to appreciate what they had or what was important.

My mother finally calmed herself. As soon as we got home, she started to prepare some of her best dishes to serve, the ones I had written to her about. I knew her goal was to fatten me up and try to restore my health. I could only take a couple bites for the food was delicious and as good as I remembered, but every bit of food seemed so rich and filling. Second, I didn't want my stomach to flare up again just when I was feeling a bit better and a little stronger.

The next morning, my dad drove to Sioux City and had me checked into St. Vincent's Hospital for further treatment. The Chancery Office and headquarters for the Diocesan Papal Volunteers was there. The irony of being back in St. Vincent, where I started my first job while studying for the Papal Volunteers, didn't escape me. I kept hoping Am from the engineering department would pop in, but that didn't happen.

The very same day, batteries of tests were conducted on me, and I could only wait as, once again, IVs were started in my arm. My lower intestine was scraped for a culture, along with all the other tests. Three days went by, and I was advised that, whatever I had, the doctors in Brazil had cured me.

The doctor who gave me the good news said, "Who better than the doctors in the country where the amoebas took control of your body than the ones to cause the cure. What you had, we have never seen before but only read about in medical school."

Weak but cured, I stopped by the Papal Volunteers office and spoke with Father Zenk. Remembering his trip down the Amazon, he somewhat knew what I went through. Father Zenk told me to go back to my folks' farm and recuperate for a month. Then we would meet again.

Home again, my dog Duke, who had stopped eating, was so happy to see me and nearly knocked me down in my weakened state. It was as if he knew I was back for good, and his health immediately improved. He started to eat again like there would never be another chance.

Everyone treated me so differently than what I remembered. Before I left, when I would start to say something, most people paid little to no attention and often would start to talk over me or about something else. But not anymore. When I would start to speak, everyone would turn his attention to me and wait for me to speak or tell more. Invariably, I could tell they expected me to say so much more or have something deep and profound to offer. I could often see the disappointment when I offered no more or very little. I was sure it puzzled them for they were sure that something bad or bizarre must have happened. I couldn't bring myself to relive the horrors of Brazil, but that wasn't the case at all. So what was it? Why couldn't I just tell it all and relate all the things I saw and did?

While I spent the next month or so at home, I did everything I pined for while in Brazil: sitting in the air-conditioning, driving the old Chevy, hugging and running with Duke, sitting under the five huge cottonwood trees in the pasture at night, listening to the wind going through the tall branches, going hunting, eating big bowls of ice cream, drinking too much beer, eating corn-fed steer steaks, taking in movies, listening to country music, and visiting with Helen, the mother of Pat who was killed while I was in Brazil, and his sister Janet. I enjoyed going to Sunday Mass with my folks and visiting with everyone who supported me and wished me well while I was in Brazil.

My dad treated me like an adult. He would ask my opinion and listen with an intent ear, like never before. I would look at my mother and tell she was trying to figure me out just by the way she was looking at me. I knew she was very proud of me, but she worried about me too. My brother Joseph would talk to me and listen as if what I said had value. My little sister, Mary Jo, just looked at me differently, and my twin brother, Darwin, just gave me space and waited. My older brother Bob had married while I was away, and of course, our relationship changed just from that aspect. My oldest brother, Jerry, had a family and wasn't around as much. My oldest sister, Marge, lived a long distance away, so I didn't get to interact with her much. I felt that everyone had changed while I was away. Everyone seemed to be in pursuit of something very elusive, and I was sure they didn't even know what it was. Sometimes, I felt very lonely again when I thought of Brazil and the Papal Volunteers.

Father Zenk contacted me after about a month and asked if I would be willing to go "on the road" and show my slides of Brazil to some of the local churches in the diocese in an effort to continue the support of the Papal Volunteers. It was a good chance for me to help spell out some of the thoughts I had in the recesses of my mind. On occasion, at some of these gatherings, there would be other Papal Volunteers from the same area of Brazil, and I would watch their slides as well as listen to their experiences. Oftentimes, I was surprised on how the other Papal Volunteers would explain their slides and experiences, and it reinforced the idea that I had all along. Everyone would have a dissimilar spin on his time in Brazil, and I realized that everyone saw it differently. Another thing that struck me was that I couldn't bring myself to show slides of the utter poverty that we sometimes saw in Brazil. I remembered too well that, when I pointed my camera at these very poor people, it wasn't something they did to themselves. When I did this, they would look at me with very sad eyes as if to say, "What are you going to do with that photo, and who are you going to show it to so all can laugh?" I just couldn't take that kind of picture, and if I did, I made sure no one was looking back at me and my camera.

I finally met with Father Zenk and told him of my decision not to return to Brazil. If I could return to my projects in Coari, maybe, but the idea of starting all over somewhere else didn't appeal to me. The job awaiting me in Belem was helping to run a co-op there, and it wasn't for me. I also told Father Zenk that I wanted to enter the seminary for the priesthood, but he flatly said no. He wisely advised me to wait at least a year before I approached the subject again.

Gradually, the stories would come, one incident at a time, but only as if a shield would prevent from telling all. How could one relate the total without being there? Some of the Papal Volunteers from Kansas and Iowa have a reunion on a yearly basis without fail, and I know why. Not only is it a chance to meet and greet each other and try to keep pace with each other's lives, but we can be with each other and talk about the past. We feel that everyone understands without qualifications or explanations. There is no need for bragging or embellishments for we feel the past when one speaks. We just know and totally understand the Brazilian culture. It is hard to see everyone getting old. Since I'm the youngest of our group, it makes it all the more difficult to see some of my colleagues pass on to their eternal reward.

EPILOGUE

Forty-four years have passed since I left Coari, Brazil, to return to the United States. With my abrupt departure, I had many unanswered questions. To start, the exact disease I suffered from during my last month in Brazil was never totally diagnosed because the American doctors had never encountered tropical illnesses of the digestive system. One doctor did suggest that he thought I had some type of hookworm of the lower intestine, but running tests for that would be unnecessary because the symptoms of my illness had cleared up. To the credit of the Brazilian doctors, I was apparently cured in Brazil.

How did the rabbit project eventually come out? When I left Coari, John had over twenty pair of rabbits out on agreement, and to my knowledge, the project was still struggling despite that fact. I always intended to ask John the outcome and if he had remained in contact with the project. But time lapsed, and then John died suddenly of a heart attack in 1995. On several occasions, I have been told that the chicken project had been a complete success for, reportedly, thousands of hybrid chickens are roaming the backyards of Brazilian homes. If that is true, it is gratifying. But there are no facts, only rumors. I intend to return to Coari shortly after the publication of this book. I didn't want to travel there before I wrote this book, as I didn't want to contaminate my memories with current events. After I do return to Brazil, I hope to publish a sequel to this first book.

The older I get, the more I realize that my experience in Brazil affected my life in many ways. I wasn't particularly reflective about those experiences as a young man, but that has changed over the years. My family participated in Papal Volunteer reunions frequently over the past forty-five years, and I remain close to that group. In recent years, we have shared more about our actual feelings and experiences during that time. It is amazing to see how we each were touched in a unique way.

When I travel to foreign lands today, I have the ability to understand and appreciate more fully the uniqueness of other cultures. I thank my stint in Brazil for that. While being in retail for thirty years as a store manager, I always found myself hiring individuals who needed a second chance, which usually worked out well for the person and the corporation. I was often an ad hoc counselor to my employees and tried to conduct my relationship with my employees in the most humane way. I learned in Brazil that God truly made each person in his image. No matter their economic circumstances, people have their own value. Over the years, I hope my example influenced my own children positively and others who knew me. Finally, I still feel the need for community involvement, and now in my retirement years, I have the time and resources to do more service.

In so many ways, I was the man who learned by raising chickens.